End of the Trail

# *End of the Trail*

by Gene Hoopes

*Illustrations by George Phippen*

**INKWELL BOOKS**
Writing-Publishing-Printing

Cover art and text ™, ®, and © 2022 by Beatrice Media, Inc., Subsidiary of Beatrice Companies, Inc. All Rights Reserved.

**Beatrice**® GENE HOOPES, and BEATRICE are Registered Trademarks of Beatrice Companies, Inc.

This book is published by Inkwell Books, under exclusive license from Beatrice Media, Inc.

First Inkwell Books printing: May 2014

Manufactured in the United States of America.

ISBN: 978-0-9766340-2-7
Library of Congress Control Number: 2018912455

Published by Inkwell Books, LLC
10632 North Scottsdale Road, Unit 695
Scottsdale, AZ 85254
Tel. 480-315-3781
E-mail info@inkwellbooksllc.com
Website www.inkwellbooksllc.com

**INKWELL BOOKS**
Writing-Publishing-Printing

TO:

One of the most colorful
characters of all history:

THE AMERICAN COWBOY

He molded his image from the raw
clay, and colored it with
his boundless imagination.

# End of the Trail

BY GENE HOOPES

*E*VERY SO OFTEN, IN THE REALM
of Western folklore, a character emerges who dominates his
background, epitomizing the earlier West and all that it stood for - its
roundups, its rough-and-tumble existence, its gunslingers and peace-
makers during an era when the right to breathe was often determined
by the swiftness of one's draw, and the niceties of deportment took
on a brutal, perhaps primordial, cast. Jim Dawson, the protagonist
of END OF THE TRAIL, is such character, salty as the whip of the
desert wind, self-complete from his solitary nights on the prairie,
stoically fearless from his brushes with the angel Death, yet containing
within himself the essential dignity, humility and humor that have
made the cowpoke the most beloved character in American literature
and moviedom, eulogized in song and story down through the decades.

Jim Dawson is the very prototype of the American cowboy, dry,
laconic, with a deep and innate understanding and decency; he is, in
addition, the storyteller superb. And certain it is that he does not lack
for material. Indeed, Jim Dawson can truthfully be said to live only for
the nighttime, when the tenderfeet gather on the porch of the Rainbow
Ranch in the shank of the evening, and it is a nice question which they
enjoyed most - their days on horseback under the Southwestern sun,
or Jim Dawson's tales of life on the range, once the sun has punched
out for the day. The reader will share their absorption as Jim recounts
the tale of Jonah the toad, delivered, in the manner of his illustrious
namesake, from the innards of a rattlesnake, and chuckle over the plight

of the Cowboys' Union organizer in "Knights of the Spur:" He will make the acquaintance of Mr. Wind, and he will follow the exploits of The Parson, that unscrupulous mountebank who roamed the gambling halls of the West, with the hot breath of the law scorching the nape of his neck. He will examine the motives of hunch-bugs, skunks, and buzzards, and shake his head over the tall tales of the legendary Foxear, tales that don elevator shoes - or boots, rather - in the retelling by Jim Dawson. He will applaud the sagacity of Slo-foot, who won his Indian bride from the trader in a manner that can only be referred to as ingenious.

Throughout the whole, Western bad-men, near-human horses, cattle stampedes, and Indian massacres blend into a composite collage of the West as it was in an earlier clay, written in a style that is, at one and the same time, disarming and heart-warming. It was a circuitous trail, which Jim Dawson had traveled when he came at last to the Rainbow Ranch with its "Lady Boss," and Gipsy Linn lent her feminine wiles to the shaping of the old wrangler's final destiny. Jim Dawson's forte was gentling horses, but the lady presented a problem which was, in its way, every bit as challenging. His manner of resolving it, and the wisdom and humor he brought to the task, make this a book not lacking in romantic interest, richly humorous and warmly satisfying.

## THE WIND AND THE TREES

There's a whisperin' in the treetops,
　　When they're kissed by the breeze.
Wonder what they're sayin' up there;
　　The wind an' the friendly trees?

Spose they're laughin', or just sighin',
　　'Cause o' the queer things they see?
Folks, with their sorrowful blunderin'
　　Must amuse the wind an' the tree.

Folks with no peace, .folks with no joy.
　　So set on their own selves to rely.
While all the trees an' the wind
　　Look up to the Power in the sky.

Seems like I can hear 'em sayin',
　　"Queer animals, them humans be.
Yep, they're shore a funny lot,"
　　Says the wind to the friendly tree.

# Contents

| | |
|---|---|
| A NEW EPOCH | 1 |
| ELECTED | 4 |
| THE MASSACRE | 9 |
| THE LADY BOSS | 13 |
| A TALE OF TWO SWELLS | 16 |
| A MARK OF DISTINCTION | 19 |
| NOT TOO BAD | 22 |
| AMAZING INDEED | 27 |
| BANDITS AHOY | 29 |
| PERFECT CONTENTMENT | 35 |
| GIFT FROM THE CLOUDS | 38 |
| IN THE LONG, LONG AGO | 40 |
| SOMEWHAT UNDESIRABLE | 43 |
| THE SUNFLOWER OMELET | 46 |
| SPEAKING OF NUTS | 50 |
| NO ORDINARY AFFAIR | 53 |
| BOOK LARNIN' | 55 |
| IN THE GLOAMING | 61 |
| KNIGHTS OF THE SPUR | 64 |
| A MODERN JONAH | 72 |
| TROTTERVILLE | 75 |
| QUITE FILLING | 78 |
| NOT WITHOUT HUMOR | 80 |
| A MATTER OF TASTE | 85 |
| NOT TOO IMPORTANT | 87 |
| THE PARSON | 90 |
| RIDERS IN THE SKY | 94 |
| A WILD RIDE | 97 |
| A SOFT ANSWER | 101 |
| A CLEAN NOSE | 103 |
| A SAD END | 107 |
| RATHER UNEXPECTED | 110 |
| CALLING IT QUITS | 112 |

# A New Epoch

WITH SEEMING RELUCTANCE, the sun had hidden a blazing face behind Black Mountain this memorable evening. For a short while it looked as though the top of that stately mass of rock was a roaring fire. Then, as the phantom fire died out, a purple veil dropped slowly down the side of the eastern range. When that had faded into the shadow of dusk, a few fleecy clouds held the last of the coloring from Nature's matchless brush. They looked like soft rose petals floating in the azure sky.

A strange and indefinable emotion had possessed Jim Dawson, as he watched the fading colors of that glorious sunset. He felt as though he was about to enter upon a new epoch in his life. And that feeling was not without foundation, for many new and fascinating experiences were soon to be his, from which he would learn much that would be to his advantage.

With a new enthusiasm, he rode out upon the long hogs-back. That low mesa was the northern entrance to the picturesque valley upon which Jim now gazed for the first time. It was a narrow valley, but many miles long. It was a peaceful looking oasis, in this rugged land, with its green fields, clumps of cottonwood and willow, now wearing their autumn dresses of soft yellow.

Although he was yet several miles from the village, Jim could see the cluster of houses which comprised this small settlement. Here and there a ranch house was evident from the smoke which drifted lazily over the treetops. As the sun sank lower on its tireless journey to foreign lands, a current of cold air drifted out of the north. At this time of year the days might be hot, but the nights were usually cold. Jim slipped into the jacket which had been tied to his saddle, and rolled a cigarette.

Jim Dawson was on his way to the desert country. He had been instructed to put up for the night at a guest ranch in Skull Valley. It was almost dark when he rode into Rainbow Ranch. A woman in boots and Levis came from the rambling stone house. She greeted him with a warm smile, as he dismounted.

With dusty Stetson in hand, Jim returned the smile and said, "I'm from the Cross Triangle outfit, an' I'd like to see the boss."

"You're looking right at her," was the soft-voiced reply.

A puzzled expression spread over Jim's bronzed features. He scratched an ear, as though he might not have heard correctly. It was a brief but awkward moment before he said, "Pardon me, ma'am, but I wasn't expectin' to find a – lady boss." Gipsy Lynn laughed, as Jim added, "You see, I'm takin' this string o' bosses down to Wickenburg. My boss tells me I might hole up for the night at Rainbow."

"And so yon may," was the cheery response. "Your boss knows that anyone from the Cross Triangle is always welcome at Rainbow. Put your horses in the corral. You'll find plenty of hay and grain in the barn. But don't be long, for supper is almost ready."

Jim fully expected to eat in the kitchen, but instead he was given a seat at the long guest table. The hostess presided with a simple grace which put everyone at ease. The conversation was lively and the meal was bountiful, Jim Dawson contributing liberally to the merriment of the occasion. Coffee was served in front of an open fire. When Jim had finished his third cup, he made his excuses.

"Seein' as how I'd like to be off 'fore sunup," he announced, "I think I'll hit the hay, if you good folks don't mind."

He was not permitted to "hit the hay," however. Gipsy Linn had conducted him to one of the guest rooms. "Now, it shore ain't what you'd call fancy," he told himself, as he pulled off his boots, "but it's mighty comfortable. Looks sort o' like a peanut 'longside the Lazy R, but it's shore homelike. Wouldn't mind hookin' up with a place like this myself."

Jim was still talking to himself when he slid into bed. "I wonder if she ain't got no help? Didn't see a sign o' nobody, 'cept the cook. Lady boss. Yep, a lady an' a boss all rolled into one, if I know anythin'. Jim Dawson, a lot o' folks has looked at you in your time, but I shore ain't recallin' anybody lookin' clean through you before. I'll bet she knows you better'n you know yourself. Ho hum! Now, I wonder —" But what Jim may have wondered was lost amid the phantoms of dreamland.

# *Elected*

$\mathcal{I}$T WAS A DELIGHTFUL MORN-
ing in early June. Jim Dawson's spirits were as exuberant as the song
of the birds in the mesquite bushes. He was whistling airily when he
started for town in the ranch car.

Presently his mood sobered, and he said to himself, "Queer, ain't it, this
business o' life? A feller gets himself fixed some place, figurin' to spend
the rest o' his days there. Then, all o' a sudden, somethin' he ain't even
dreamed on pops up out o' nowheres. Seemed like a bumblebee in a clover
patch couldn't been more contented, but here he is, on the wing agin.

"Oh, well, 1 reckon that's one o' them things what makes life so inter-
estin'. That an' meetin' up with folks. 'Specially folks what's different, folks
what can clean some o' the cobwebs out o' a feller's head."

He fe1 1 to musing upon his own most recent experience. It seemed but
yesterday, yet a year and a half had slipped by since the day he had first
ridden down this same dusty road.

No doubt Jim's good spirits were heightened this morning because he
was on his way to meet a very old friend. This friend, whom he had not
seen for some years, was a noted doctor from the far East. He had spent
several vacations at the Lazy R. Therefore, it was quite a surprise to learn
that Dr. James Lodge was now booked for Rainbow.

"Jim," the doctor had remarked, as he settled himself in the front seat of
the car, "I see there is no need for me to inquire concerning your physical
condition. You are a living picture of good .health. I seem to detect a

slight change, however. You look happier than when I last saw you. Your new location must be to your liking."

"Doc Jimmie," was the smiling response, "you're right as four aces. It's all to my likin', shore 'nough."

"Well, I'm certainly glad to hear that," the doctor returned. "When I learned the Lazy R had been sold I was much concerned about you. I knew how well-satisfied you were with the Steams, and I couldn't think of you being contented anyplace else. Henry wrote to me from California, telling me where you were. And since I've wanted to have a look at Arizona for a long time, I decided to come out and check up on you. I made a reservation for only two weeks, but if I like the place I may stay all summer. I retired last year, so I'm as free as a bird now."

"Well, I can tell you one thing," was Jim's prompt response. "You ain't apt to be needin' two weeks to make up your mind concernin' Rainbow. If you stay two days, you're lost."

"Now, just how should I take that?" the doctor laughingly inquired. "I hadn't planned on getting lost, you know."

"Oh, I'll see that you don't go astray, Doc. What I meant was that if you stay two days, you're mighty apt to be stayin' all summer. I'll lay a couple o' bucks that the Lady Boss has you eatin' out o' her hand in twenty-four hours."

"Lady Boss," the doctor repeated. "Don't tell me this place is being operated by a woman I"

"Correct as the movin' o' the stars, Doc. An' you're goin' to admit 'fore them two days is gone that she knows how to operate it, or my name ain't Dawson. I'm tellin' you that gal has a way with her. She shore knows how to make the dudes comfortable an' happy."

"Well, that sounds encouraging, at least. But tell me, Jim, how you came to locate here. Had you heard of the place before you came down?"

"Nope," was the drawling reply, "hadn't never heard o' Rainbow Ranch, an' hadn't never seen Skull Valley. Knew there was such a place ''cause I punched cattle over in the Verde country a good many years ago.

"Nope, my hookin' up with Rainbow was what a feller might call a happenstance, if you get my meanin'. It sort o' seemed like I didn't have nothin' to do with it."

"For the love of St. Patrick," the doctor shouted, "keep your hands on that wheel, man!" Jim had elected to roll a cigarette while they were drifting down the mountain to the hog back.

"Don't be scared, Doc. This car's well broke. An' you'll soon get used to these hills." Silence followed that consoling remark.

When they were safely off the mountain, the doctor heaved a sigh of relief, and said, "Now go on with your story, Jim. It may help to quiet my nerves."

'Well, to begin at the beginnin', it was like this. I hated to admit it, but I was gettin' sort o' tired o' the rough winters up north. A bad sign, mebbe, but that's how it was. When Henry sells out I figure it's a good time for yours truly to be shovin' south. I'm cravin' a climate where I ain't havin' to pack a load o' heavy garments through a long winter.

"Now I ain't never seen this section o' the state, so I figure to have me a look-see. An' I ain't in town but two days when I hear the Cross Triangle outfit is lookin' for a wrangler. I tie into that job pronto, 'cause the feller what runs the dude business operates in Wickenburg durin' the winter.

"Well, the Cross Triangle closes a couple o' weeks after I land. Then the boss gives me the job o' movin' the hosses down to the desert. It's a three-day trip, an' I've got orders to hole up in Skull Valley for the first night. Now it's 'most nigh dark when I pull into Rainbow Ranch. But I can see 'nough o' the place to make me scratch my head. I was sort o' wok back, you might say. Rainbow didn't look much bigger'n a cup o' tea. Comparin' it with the Lazy. R, that is.

"Then I was shore set back on my hind legs," Jim continued, with a broad grin, "when I bump into the Lady Boss. But the shock don't last long. She greets me like I'm a ol' friend. What's more, she treats me like

I'm the Prince o' Pilsner, or somethin' besides what I am.

"Anyways, I don't recall ever eatin' a better. meal, nor sleepin' in a better bed. I call it a day right soon after supper. An' when the Lady Boss shows me my room I don't say good night . I thank her for treatin' me so royal-like, an' say good-by. That's 'cause I figure to be on my way 'fore she's up. But I figured wrong.

"I feed the hosses 'bout daybreak. An' seein' a light in the kitchen, I figure to get me a cup o' coffee 'fore I pull out. But the cook ain't up yet. It's the Lady Boss, an' she's got breakfast waitin' for me. An' while I'm stowin' 'way a stack o' hot cakes, she tells me 'bout the trouble she's had with wranglers.

" 'So,' says she, 'if you hear o' a reliable man, I'll be mighty grateful if you can send him this way.' 'What sort o' feller might you have in mind?' I asked her. She laughs, an' says, 'The kind what ain't generally runnin' 'round loose. For one thing, he must be a stranger to liquor. But more'n that, he must be kind to hosses, an' considerate o' the guests. I don't tum my guests over to some fresh cowpoke for his amusement. There's too much o' that nonsense in this business.'

"Now I agree with her, an' tell her I'll keep my eyes an' ears open. Well, Doc, I ain't too shore yet what got into me. 'Course, I done a heap o' thinkin' that day. An' the more I thought on it, the less I was bothered 'bout the size o' that place. Now, much as I liked the Lazy R, it seemed like there was somethin' lackin' there. Mebbe it was too big – I dunno. Anyways, it looked to me like a feller could get to know folks a heap better, if there wasn't so many to look after.

"So, by the time I get down to Wickenburg my ballot is made out. An' in less'n a week after I'd left Rainbow I was back there, ready to cast my vote. The Lady Boss was feedin' the hosses when I ride up to the corral that evenin'. She didn't look a mite surprised when she saw me.

" 'Well, ma'am,' says I, 'mebbe I didn't use my eyes an' ears as well as I might, but I done the best I knew. I couldn't find but one feller what seemed like he might fit your specifications for a wrangler. I took no chances on him goin' astray, so I come 'long with him. An' I'm recommendin' him for the job. He ain't young, but he knows the game, an' he's steady. His name's Jim Dawson.'

"Well, Doc, it would shore warmed your heart, if you'd heard the Lady Boss laugh. She give me her hand, an' says, 'I've been lookin' for just such a man for a long time. An' I accept your recommendation. Jim Dawson is elected.'"

# The Massacre

THE DUDES HAD DISMOUNTED in a shady spot near Castle Rock this afternoon, where they had a wonderful view of the valley below.

"Oh, how lovely!" one of the women exclaimed.

"Yes, isn't it?" another agreed. "But what a horrible name to give it."

"Perhaps our genial guide can tell us how it came to be called Skull Valley," one of the men remarked. "How about it, Jim?"

"Well," Jim replied, as he eased onto his bootheels, "I can only tell you what I've heard. I don't know if it's a fact, 'course, but this is the story they tell 'round here. Seems like a scoutin' party was sent out o' Fort Whipple one time – but they never come back. 'Course, that wasn't nothin' unusual in them days, with Injuns on the warpath a good part o' the time.

"Quite a spell after that, another party from Whipple wanders down here. They find the whole valley littered with bleached skulls an' bones. They figure this is where their comrades has been massacred, so they call the place Skull Valley. But that story ain't as satisfyin' as the one ol' Foxear tells. Leastwise, to me it ain't." Jim began to roll a cigarette, as though he intended keeping that story for another occasion.

"Well, let us have it, Jim," one of his friends demanded.

"Now, ol' Foxy says what these folks tell might be all right as far as it goes," Jim began, when the cigarette had been lighted. "But he claims that ain't the half o' it. He says he was down in this country long 'fore white men ever stumbled into it.

The Massacre

"The Yavapais was livin' here them days, an' Foxy claims skulls was most nigh as thick as polliwogs in a rain barrel. 'Course, I don't reckon many o' you folks ever seen a rain barrel. Anyways, Foxear asks one o' his friends 'bout it one time, an' this is the story he got.

"Seems like these Yavapais was travelin' on crocodiles when they move up here from the south."

"Crocodiles!" someone exclaimed. "Why, I never heard of such a thing."

"Mebbe not, Miss," Jim calmly replied. "But I reckon the Injun did a lot a' things we ain't never heard 'bout. Them fellers never took up the habit o' tellin' everythin' they knowed. An', you see, this was long 'fore the Injuns had ever seen a hoss.

"Now, in some ways, them crocodiles was better'n bosses. A half dozen Injuns could ride on a full-growed crocodile. Anyways, that's the way it was, cordin' to ol' Foxy. Comin' up off the desert in the summertime, this valley looks mighty good to them Yavapai folks. They was right fond o' farmin', them days. An' here was good soil, an' a right smart creek runnin' down the valley.

"So that Yavapai outfit decides to settle down here. They build 'em a dam in the creek so the crocodiles can have a place to frolic. An' then they build 'em a house. They was a peaceful lot, them Injuns was. The whole tribe live in one big house.

"Now, Foxy says this house was two stories high. It's built like a fort, 'cause them fellers knowed there was plenty o' redskins what didn't believe in peace. Their livin' quarters is on the second floor. The ground floor is where they store their com an' meat. An' bein' as how t hey like to take a trip up into the hills now an' agin, they always have some o' them croco- diles cooped up there, handy-like.

"Well, they've been here quite a spell, when a band o' Apaches swoop down on 'em onc day. Foxy says the Yavapais was outnumbered a hundred to one. But they was mighty good with a bow an' arrow, them Yavapais was. An' behind that fort they shore cut down the odds.

12

"But the Apaches keep comin', an' it looks mighty desperate to them Yavapais. That is, till somebody hatches a big idee. The chief gives the order, an' them braves just pack up their arrows an' move downstairs. Now it's so quiet all o' a sudden that the Apaches figure it's all over. An' they don't lose no time gettin' ready to move in.

"But – when the Yavapais come ridin' out on them crocodiles, the Apaches knowed they'd figured wrong. You see, this the first time they ever lay eyes on a crocodile. An' when they see them critters' jaws open up like the gates o' hell, they shore ain't waitin' to ask no questions.

"Foxy says it was one awful slaughter. He says even when he was here the Yavapais was still usin' them skulls to keep the crows out o' their cornfields."

# The Lady Boss

OCTOR JIMMIE WAS TAKING
a stroll about the ranch this afternoon, with Mike at his heels. This
fine-looking bull terrier was the ranch mascot. Did Mike consider it
his duty to protect the guests, or was he fearful lest they appropriate
something which did not belong to them? That was an unanswerable
question, of course. But, no matter how friendly he might be, he kept a
watchful eye upon them at all times.

The doctor's stroll finally took him to the bunkhouse, where he found
his friend Jim Dawson cleaning saddles in the shade of a cottonwood.
He sat down on a bench and began to pack his pipe. Jim eased onto his
bootheels, and took the Durham from his shirt pocket.

"Don't let me interfere with your duties, Jim. I can always enjoy watching
a fellow work; especially when I feel disinclined myself."

"Oh, I reckon I can take time out to be a bit sociable," was Jim's prompt
response. Then, after a brief silence, "Well, Doc, do you think you can
make it?"

"Make what?"

"Why, them two weeks you booked for. Think you can stick it out that
long?"

"Well, I've been here three days," the doctor returned, as he lit his pipe.
"Have you heard me complaining?"

"Nope. But that ain't answerin' my question. An' I reckon you know by
this time I ain't too long on askin' questions."

"Well, my friend," was the thoughtful response, "I don't mind making a confession to you. In all my travels I never found such a place as this. I feel perfectly at home here. There is an air of peace and harmony about this place which defies description. Even the animals seem influenced by it." The doctor paused to gaze at the dog stretched out so contentedly at his feet. "Yes, Jim, I think you can count on me sticking around for the balance of the season."

"Now that's shore good news," was Jim's warm response. " 'Cause it means you'll be here for quite a spell. You see, Rainbow ain't got no regular season like the Lazy R. Weather bein' what it is down here, we're open most all year."

Doctor Jimmie gazed thoughtfully across the valley. "But to go back for a moment," he finally said. "I suppose it isn't always so peaceful. You probably have guests who are not able to appreciate it, and are therefore more or less disturbing."

"Oh, shore," Jim chawled, with an odd smile. "Now an' agin we get some like that. But they never stay long 'nough. to do much disturbin'. The Lady Boss takes care o' that right neatly." Silence followed. Jim snuffed the cigarette, and returned to his work.

"Gipsy," the doctor mused, slowy stroking his chin. "Gipsy Lynn." Jim turned inquiring eyes upon his friend.

"Was you speakin' to me, or Mike?" he asked.

"To neither of you – intentionally," the doctor slowly replied. "I must have been thinking out loud. Thinking about your Lady Boss, and her unusual name."

"Well, she ain't no usual person." And with that stout declaration Jim sat down again, and rolled another cigarette.

"Yes, I agree with you, Jim. She is indeed a rare individual. And I'm very glad to see that you appreciate that fact."

"Why, Doc," was the prompt return, "I didn't think there was room in my ol' head for the things I've learned from that gal. An' I don't mind doin' a little confessin' myself. Gipsy Lynn's the finest woman I ever met up with."

"I appreciate your confidence, Jim. And I suppose you have made your confession to the lady also."

"Mike, get them cows out o' here!" Some stray cattle were lazily plodding up the road which led to the ranch house. With a yip of delight, Mike was off in a cloud of dust. Doctor Jimmie roared as he watched the faithful dog send those trespassers flying to safer quarters.

"Now, Jim," the doctor said, when all was quiet again, "I would like an answer to *my* question. I don't mean to be curious, but I am interested in your welfare. Have you told your Lady Boss what you just told me?"

"I should say not." "May I ask why?"

" 'Cause, I ain't quite that simple-minded," Jim drawled. "I know when I'm well off. Anyways, I've got a hunch I know 'bout what she'd be sayin', if I got that fresh. She'd most likely say to me, 'Jim, I can see you've had somethin' to eat what ain't agreed with you. Excuse me while I fix you a dose o' salts'."

# A Tale of Two Swells

A YOUNG LADY ON HER FIRST visit to the West said to Jim Dawson one day, "Are the stories one hears about rattlesnakes really true?"

"Well, Miss," Jim returned, with the suspicion of a grin, "I reckon that sort o' depends on who's doin' the tellin'." The questioner's face wore a puzzled expression, but she was silent.

It was one of the older patrons of Rainbow who kept the subject alive. "Jim, I presume that snake story of yours was true. I mean the one where you entertained the rattlers by whistling Yankee Doodle."

"Oh, shore," was Jim's smiling response.

"Perhaps Miss – would like to hear that one."

"Yes, indeed I would," was the eager suggestion.

"Oh, there wasn't nothin' to that story, Miss. But if you're shore you want a honest-to-Henry snake story, I'll give you the one I heard my granddad tell onct."

"Yes, please do," came from several of the dudes who were lolling about in the refreshing shade. Jim rolled a cigarette.

"Now, folks," he finally began, "I ain't vouchin' for the truth o' this here story I'm 'bout to give you. I'm only the middleman, you might say. I reckon the best part o' it is that it ain't costin' you nothin'.

"Well, I've heard as how animals swells up somethin' terrible when they're hit by a rattlesnake. But I ain't never seen it myself, so I wouldn't know. 'Course, way back in them early days mebbe the rattlers was a heap worse'n they is now. 'Cardin' to some o' the old-timers, they must've been.

"Now when I was a kid there wasn't nothin' I liked better'n hearin' bout the good ol' days. 'Cept goin' swimmin', 'course. Granddad an' his crony, Soupbone, was talkin' 'bout rattlesnakes one day. Soupbone says when he first come to Texas, rattlers was most nigh as thick as fleas on a dog's tail. He tens as how they'd brung a cow an' some pigs with 'em. An' they'd scarce got located, he says, when one o' them pesky rattlers up an' hits the cow.

" 'Well,' says Soupbone, 'that critter starts swellin'. An' she keeps right on swellin' for three whole days. I'm wonderin' what I'm goin' do with her when I get me one o' them high-polished ideas o' mine. Get 'em every now an' agin', you know. You see, we ain't had no time to fix a place for the pigs, an' they was givin' us a heap o' trouble. So, when Mrs. Cow quits swellin' I get me a stout stick, an' props her jaws open. Now that makes a right smart door, considerin' I don't have to buy no hinges. An' for a long spell – now let's see, it must've been ten or twelve years – the pigs lived in that ol' carcass, snug as lice in a hencoop.'

"Granddad, he laughs right hearty, an' starts packin' his pipe agin. I figure Soupbone has the ol' boy stopped on that one. But that's only 'cause o' me still havin' much to learn 'bout my granddad. For a spell it looks like the ol' boy ain't goin' to offer no defense. An' that shore wasn't like Granddad. So Soupbone says, 'Mebbe you ain't minded to believe that story.' 'Shore, I'm believin' it,' says Granddad. 'Ain't got no reason to be doubtin' it. But that wasn't nothin'.' Then he tells this one.

" 'When I was a young feller,' he says, 'I lived in Colorado for a spell. One day durin' the fall roundup I trailed a bunch o' steers into one o' them box-canyons. Hadn't more'n got started into that crack in the mountain when a rattler pops out o' nowheres. 'Fore I can whip out the six-shooter he's snapped his jaws onto my hoss' hind leg. 'Course, I don't waste no time blastin' the insides out o' that cussed varmint. But that ain't helpin' the hoss none. He just stretches out, groans a couple o' times, an' starts swellin'. Seein' I can't do him no good, I figure I might as well see how much stock I got corraled in that canyon.'

" 'Now it's a long canyon, but I ain't gone much more'n a hour,' says he. 'But when I get back I find I'm trapped. Yep, I'm trapped in that place like a ant in a sugar bowl. That hoss had already swelled up till there wasn't no way out, an' he keeps on swellin' for days an' days.'

" 'Well,' Granddad rambles on, 'one hot afternoon I was takin' me a siesta in the shade o' a big rock when the explosion come. Thought the whole mountain was comin' down on me. Couldn't figure it out for a minute or so. Then it come to me. The hide on that poor hoss o' mine had got tired o' stretchin', an' let loose. Now I knowed them steers wouldn't be goin' near that mess, so there wasn't no call to be botherin' 'bout them. So I crawl out, an' drag my weary bones nine miles to the ranch. Next day the whole crew was put to work clearin' the mouth o' that canyon so's we could get the steers out. If my memory ain't got wobbly, there was seven in the crew, an' they wasn't no weaklin's, neither. We worked from sunup till dark, an' it took nigh onto two weeks to get them steers out o' there.' "

# A Mark of Distinction

*W*HEN THE JENKINS' MADE
their first visit to Rainbow, it was with considerable uncertainty. Mrs.
Jenkins' experience with riding schools had been anything hut reassuring.
She was a lover of animals, yet had a strange timidity regarding horses.
It was not fear of the horse itself, but, as she expressed it, "When I'm in
the saddle I feel so far up in the air that I become panicky."

When Jim Dawson heard this, he said, "Now, ma'am, you just slip into
your ridin' togs, an' I'll introduce you to a hoss what'll make you forget
that feelin', or my name ain't Dawson."

Four horses were saddled when the Jenkins reported a short while
later. The blue eyes which were turned upon Jim Dawson were plainly
troubled, however. "Now, ma'am," he said, with a reassuring smile, "come
an' meet the hoss what's goin' to give you the best ride you ever had."
He led her to a small bay horse. "Paddy, this is Mrs. Jenkins. She's a mite
nervous concernin' hosses. But I know you can show her she ain't got
nothin' to worry 'bout."

Mrs. Jenkins timidly stroked the horse's glossy neck. But when Paddy
touched her shoulder with his nose she threw her arms about his neck
with an exclamation of delight. By that one affectionate gesture Paddy
had gained her confidence. When Mrs. Jenkins was in the saddle and the
stirrups had been adjusted, Jim asked, "Do you feel like you was sittin' on
a skyscraper now?"

"I certainly don't," was the enthusiastic return.

"An' I can promise you," Jim said, "that you're just as .safe up there as if you was in your mother's arms. All you got to do is keep a light rein, an' tell Paddy what you want; he'll understand. Now, Paddy, you show the lady that gentlemen ain't all built with only two legs." Gipsy joined them at that moment, and they were off.

When they returned, Mrs. Jenkins face was flushed, and her eyes were dancing. "Oh, that was a wonderful ride!" she exclaimed, as she dismounted. "I didn't have the slightest uneasiness, because Paddy seemed to know just what I wanted of him."

"Shore he did," was .Jim's smiling response. "You can always depend on Paddy."

"Yes, he certainly is a four-legged gentleman. What's more, I'm in love with him already. Where did you ever find such a horse, or did you raise him yourself?"

"Nope, I bought him 'bout a year ago."

"Had you known him before that?"

"Nope, hadn't never seen the little feller before." Admiring eyes were following Paddy's every move. "How did you ever find such a horse?" Mrs. Jenkins asked, after a brief pause.

"Well, we was needin' another reliable hoss. We have some mighty good hosses, but there was only one what you might call foolproof. Most hosses don't like totin' tender-foots you know. Sort o' hurts their pride, I reckon. So, as I said, we was Jookin' for another foolproof boss.

"Now I hear 'bout this feller, so I go have me a look. An' I don't have to look long 'fore I'm mighty shore Paddy belongs to the Rainbow string."

"But," Mrs. Jenkins persisted, "how could you possibly know that he was such a reliable animal – foolproof, as yOu call it?"

"Well, ma'am, I'll show you." Jim raised the horse's head, and put a finger on his chin. "See that? Sort o' funny too, how so few folks seems to know 'bout it. But I'm tellin' you, ma'am, it's most nigh like findin' gold. When you're lookin' for a hoss what's reliable, an' shore 'nough gentleman, be shore he's got a wart on his chin."

# Not Too Bad

$\mathcal{T}$HE RIDERS WERE TAKING
their ease in the shadow of Castle Rock this morning. Mrs. Jenkins had
discovered a clump of grama grass hiding among the rocks, and was
now feeding it to her pet, Paddy.

Mr. Jenkins, sitting beside Jim Dawson, watched his wife with admiring
eyes. "I suppose," he casually remarked, "one would have to pay a right
good price for a horse like Paddy."

"Oh, not too much," was the drawling return, while Jim scratched the
ears of the faithful Mike. A brief silence followed.

"No doubt," was Mr. Jenkins' next comment, "horses bring more over
on the coast than they do here."

"Could be," came from Jim, as he began to roll a cigarette. With a rather
grim expression on his face, Mr. Jenkins joined his wife.

It was late that same afternoon when Mr. Jenkins made his way to the
corral. His ruddy countenance wore a troubled expression, as he spread
his arms on the corral fence. Silently, he puffed a cigarette, the while he
watched Jim Dawson. He was not a lone spectator, however. The horses
too had their heads over the fence eagerly watching their master filling
their feed-boxes with sweet-smelling hay.

When the corral gate had finally been opened, Jim came to lean against
the fence while he rolled a cigarette. Mr. Jenkins cast a puzzled glance at
the wranglee, but continued to smoke in silence. A slight frown creased
his brow, as his gaze was turned upon the feeding horses.

"Jim," he finally said, with unaccustomed abruptness, "what will you take for Paddy?"

With the cigarette in one band and a lighted match in the other, Jim looked sharply at his companion. Then he grinned, as he replied, "Who told you he was for sale?"

"No one," was the gloomy return. "But let's not waste time bickering. We want that horse, or I should say, my wife does. We're leaving in the morning. And she's going to be a mighty unhappy woman unless she knows Paddy will soon be following her. I'll give you a hundred dollars for him, and I imagine that's a lot more than he's worth."

"Might be," Jim drawled. "But it don't make much difference, seein' as how the boss ain't for sale.'

"Oh, come now, be reasonable. You know you can get another horse for half what I'm offering you."

"Shore, but not one like Paddy."

"Well, couldn't you stretch a point for a friend? I'm in_ a jam. I promised the wife I would buy Paddy for her. And you know how it is with women, Jim, when they don't get what they have their hearts set on."

"Nope, can't say as I do. You see, I ain't had no experience 'long that line. Hosses is my specialty."

Jenkins was forced to smile. But his voice had not lightened any when he said, 'I'll raise the offer to one-fifty."

"Well, my friend," Jim replied, as his gaze wandered to the feeding horses, "that ain't a bad price for 'most any hoss. An' it would pleasure me to do you a favor. But you see, when I said Paddy ain't for sale, I wasn't kiddin'." With a hopeless shrug Jenkins turned to go, but Jim was speaking again.

"Now it's like this. Mebbe I don't look it, but I'm human. An' I got a lot o' feelin' when it comes to animals – 'specially hosses. Often wonder if I might o' been one myself sometime. A feller can't be too shore 'bout them things, you know." He paused a moment, scratching an ear. "Well, anyways, I've give my word to Paddy, an' I aim to keep it."

"I don't get you, Jim."

"Well, I'll try agin." Jim smiled. "Now, it don't take me all summer to see as how life for that little hoss shore ain't been what you might call a bed o' violets. Hard work an' mighty little kindness had been his lot. An' havin' had some experience 'long that line myself, I was right shore how he felt when he found himself with folks what wasn't too self-minded to remember he had feelin's, too.

"Well, he was such a faithful little feller, an' so happy here, that I made him a promise. I told him he was fixed for the rest o' his days. Yep, as long as Jim Dawson was kickin', he had nothin' to worry 'bout. That's the way it is 'tween me an' Paddy. An' if you was to offer me a thousand for him, I'd still have to say, 'Thanks much, but no deal'."

Mr. Jenkins had been telling the guests about his unsuccessful attempt to purchase Paddy when Jim came around the comer of the ranch house that evening. Taking his usual seat on the veranda steps, he laid the timeworn guitar beside him. Then, with an appreciative glance at Black Mountain, now tinted by the afterglow of sunset, he began to roll a cigarette. It was Doctor Jimmie wh0 broke the silence.

"Jim," he remarked, "I understand that good horses command rather high prices out in this country."

"So far as I know," Jim replied, with a suspicious glance at his friend, "there ain't no set price on hosses, good or bad."

"I'm no horseman, of course," the doctor ventured, "but it would seem to me that a thousand dollars was a lot of money for one horse. Wasn't that what you refused for your Paddy?"

"Nope. It wasn't offered, so I couldn't refuse it. I just said I'd have to turn it down, if it was offered."

"But you don't have a lot of money tied up in the animal, do you?"

"Not too much."

"My, but you're a confidential cuss," the doctor commented, as he relit his pipe.

It was Gipsy who broke a rather awkward silence which had followed the doctor's last remark. "I can understand Jim's feeling in the matter. For I'm quite certain I couldn't put a price on anything I loved. But I do think you should satisfy the folks' curiosity, Jim. Since you have no intention of selling the horse, you might tell them what he cost you.."

A roar of laughter followed Jim's drawling answer. He picked up the guitar, as he said, "Somethin' less'n twenty-five bucks."

"Why, man, you didn't buy the horse," Doctor Jimmie exclaimed, "you stole him!"

"Nope, I shore 'nough bought him," was the calm return. "Paid hard cash, too."

"What did you give beside the cash?" someone asked. "Nothin'.."

"Come now, Jim, tell us how you managed it."

"Oh, it didn't take much managin'," Jim slowly replied, with half-closed eyes. "You see, we was needin' another hoss, an' I beard 'bout one down the valley bein' for sale. So I figure to have me a look. I don't know the feller what owns him.

" 'Howdy,' says I. 'Hear you got a hoss you'd like to unload on a tender-foot.' 'You got it straight,' says he. 'That's the boss over there. Get down, an' have a look at one o' the best cow ponies in these parts.'

"Well, when I see that poor critter standin' under a tree, with his chin 'most nigh touchin' the ground, I figure I've seen a-penty. But since I ain't pushed for time, I reckoned I could be a bit neighborly. The hoss is saddled, an' the feller tells me he was just leavin' to round up some stray calves. An' I'm wonderin' how far he figures on gettin' with that pack o' bones. The hoss don't look like he'd had a square meal since the last election. He don't even blink when we come up to him.

" 'Hi, feller,' says I. Then he picks up his head, an' turns them big brown eyes on me. It's sort o' like he's sayin', 'Would you know where a feller could find a friend?' Mebbe that look sort o' got me, 'cause I come 'most nigh tellin' him he's already found one. Anyways, he's got me interested, so I look him over right careful.

"Now, he shore ain't young, an' as I said, he's mighty forlorn lookin'. But, I'm thinkin' to myself, he wouldn't be a bad lookin' hoss with a couple o' weeks' full rations, an' the cockleburs worked out o' his mane an' tail He's sound, an' he's got a head full o' good sense.

" 'Feet in bad shape,' says I, 'but that ain't his fault. What you askin' for him?'

" 'Twenty-five bucks,' the feller says.

" 'Twenty-five – as is?' I say to him, sort o' careless-like. I see a couple o' pieces o' balin' wire is holdin' the bridle together. An' the saddle looks like it might been made 'bout the time o' the Civil War.

"The feller scratches hi head, then he says, Well, 1 hadn't figured on givin' the hoss away. But I ain't got no real need for him. Shore, neighbor, if you want the outfit for twenty-five bucks, it's yours. But I'm speakin' o' cash on this deal.'

" 'I don't deal in nothin' but,' says I. Then I stuff five o' Uncle Sam's five spots into the feller's itchin' paw. I hitch the reins 'round the saddle horn, an' rub Paddy's nose. 'Come 'long, M'Guire,' says I, 'we're goin' home.' I throw a leg over Lady, an' we're off. Paddy, he come trottin' after us with his ears up, an' lookin' like he'd just got a first mortgage on life."

"I suppose you didn't discover the wart on Paddy's nose until afterward," Mrs. Jenkins remarked.

"Oh, shore, that was one o' the first things I run onto. When I found that, the feller could have had a hundred bucks, as easy as twenty-five."

"Then you probably felt you had made quite a good deal," came from another guest.

"Yep," Jim drawled, gazing up at the stars, "seein' as how I got ten bucks for the ol' saddle, I figured mebbe I'd done right well."

# Amazing Indeed

*J*IM DAWSON HAD TAK.EN THE dudes up to a spur of the mountain near Panther Gulch this morning. They had halted in the shade of a big cedar for a few minutes' rest.

In the party was a young woman from the far East who almost boastingly admitted that this was the first time she had been farther west than the Allegheny Mountains. Naturally, she was quite curious concerning the many strange sights which confronted her in this vast new land.

Most of the dudes had dismoilnted, but this one sat in her saddle, staring intently up the long valley. "Mr. Dawson," she finally asked, "what is that queer-lookino- thing up there?"

Jim's lazy eyes followed her gaze. "Well, Miss," he answered, "there's a lot o' things out there. There's a bunch o' cattle over there, Iayin' in the shade o' them mesquite bushes. An' there's a jackrabbit sittin' over there by the wash, sctatchin' his left ear. Just what was you referrin' to?"

"That thing away up there, whirling in the sunlight."

"Oh, that." There was the merest suspicion of a grin about Jim's generous mouth. He extracted the Bull Durham from his pocket before answering. "Well, Miss, that ain't nothin' but a windmill."

"A windmill," she repeated, with a puzzled look.

"Yep. Ain't you never seen a windmill 'fore?"

"No, I never have," was the hesitant reply. "They are used for pumping water, are they not?"

"That's right," was the drawling reply, as Jim lit the cigarette. "Generally speakin', that is. They come in mighty handy for coolin' too."

"Cooling? I don't believe I understand." She slid stiffly to the ground.

"Well, back where you come from I reckon you use them 'lectric fans to keep from boilin' over in summer."

"Yes, of course."

"But out here," Jim explained, "them toys wouldn't do much good. You see, these windmills is a hundred times bigger, an' they shore stir up a breeze. There's another one down at the south end o' the valley. That's how we keep it cool out here."

"Cool!" someone exclaimed. "Why, it must be a hundred in the shade right now."

"Mebbe so," Jim admitted. "But if it wasn't for them windmills it might be a hundred an' fifty."

"Amazing," was all the first dude could say, as she fanned her face with her new Stetson.

"Yep," Jim agreed. "I reckon it is sort o' amazin', when you come to think on it."

# Bandits Ahoy

"IT WAS A WARM EVENING; the usual chill had not yet descended upon the valley. The dudes were grouped about the patio watching Black Mountain, as it was slowly enveloped in the shadows of night.

The silence was finally broken by one of Jim Dawson's long-time friends. "Jim," he said, "I've listened to a great many of your stories. Yet in none of them have I ever heard you mention bandits. Did you never encounter any of those predatory specimens in the old days?"

"Pre – which?" Jim inquired, scratching an ear.

"Perhaps that was a poor choice of words, so we'll skip it," his friend laughingly replied. "I was referring to those who are sometimes called holdup artists."

"Oh, you mean outlaws," Jim returned. "Shore, I used to meet up with some o' them coyotes now an' agin. Nothin' ever callin' for shootin' -irons, though. Seemed like I was always lucky 'nough to be somewheres else when them varmints was ridin' herd. Come mighty near messin' with 'em onct. Missed it by a eyelash, you might say."

"Would you mind telling us about it?" someone asked.

"Nope, I don't mind. You might, though, 'cause it ain't apt to be too interestin'. Anyways, here it is. This goes way back to that time I was scoutin' for the army. The boys hadn't got but one pay all that winter. Spring was 'bout to bud, an' another pay was long past due.

"Well, one night the colonel sends for me. 'Dawson,' .says he, 'last week's mail tells me our pay was to be shipped on the sixteenth. That bein' so, it could be here on the twentieth – that's day after tomorrow.' 'I've got both ears open, Colonel,' says I, rollin' me a cigarette. 'Well,' says he, 'you'll be needin' more'n your ears on the job I'm hand-in' you. You're mighty apt to be needin' both hands, 'long with your ears. You're goin' to Hartersville tomorrow. Put your hoss up an' do a bit o' snoopin' to get the lay o' things, if you can. Then you're returnin' on the stage to keep a eye -on that money.'

" 'I just got a tip today,' the colonel tells me, 'as how Copper Hilton is figurin' to relieve us o' that money some-wheres 'tween here an' Hartersville.'

"Well, I reckon my mouth was hangin' open 'bout that time. Anyways, I says, 'You expectin' me to do that job single-handed, Colonel?' 'That's exactly what I'm expectin', Dawson,' he hands back to me. 'I could send a troop to guard the stage, but I got my reasons for not doin' so. You see, I don't want nobody knowin' as how I've got this information.

" 'Now, Dawson,' he gives me, 'you're the best two-gun flinger in these parts. An' I want that buzzard Hilton dropped in his tracks. That outlaw is already late for his meetin' with St. Peter. An' if anybody can bust that gang 'fore it gets, started, it's Jim Dawson. You've got your orders-an' luck to you. But don't show up here without that money.'

"Well, I don't seem to sleep too comfortable that night. But I'm on my way to Hartersville first thing next mornin'. I put my hoss up at Jake Plummer's livery barn. Jake's a Texan, an' a ol' friend o' mine. " 'Well, Jake,' says I, 'what's new?' 'Nothin' I knows on,' says Jake. 'Nothin' stewin' lately?' I ask, sort o' like I ain't carin' much. 'Well,' says Jake, " 'a feller can't never be too shore. Young Hilton busts into town this mornin'. Most generally that means somethin' worse'n squally weather.' 'That's all I want,' says I. 'Take good care o' the hoss, Jake. See you tomorrow.' Now Jake's wife run a boardin' house, so I amble over there an' get me a room.

"It's too early to eat, so I stretch me out on the bed, an do a bit o' thinkin'. Fact is, I been at that job most o' the day. An' the more I'm thinkin' on it the less I'm likin' this army business. It's got so I ain't too pleased with it. An' it looks like this might be a right good time to chuck it. While the chuckin' is offered, you might say.

"Yep, I'm thinkin', I shore couldn't be no worse off doin' a lot o' things I could mention. I might even go in for farmin'. Know a nice hunk o' land south o' Dogtown what a feller can pick up cheap. Nope, it might not be so bad, thinks I. Leastwise, I wouldn't be forever riskin' my hide bein' shot full o' holes.

"Now this Hilton what Jake mentions so respectful-like is Copper's younger brother. I've seen him a couple o' times, an' he's shore a ugly lookin' varmint. So, he's in town. Well, that shore looks like the colonel's tip was hot off the griddle. An' somehow or other that farmin' notion o' mine gets to lookin' more temptin' every minute." The dudes waited patiently while Jim rolled a cigarette.

"Well," he finally continued, "after I get me some sup-per, I slide into the Bighorn. An' the first feller I see, with his hoof on the rail, is this young Hilton. 'Howdy,' says he, when I ease up to the bar. Now that buzzard ain't never spoke to me 'fore now. What's the game, I'm wonderin'. But I says to him, 'Oh, 'bout as good as a thirsty man could be, I reckon.' 'It's on me, then,' says he, with a laugh what shore ain't too pleasant.

"I'm shore tempted to scratch my head 'bout then, but I don't. I hear Hilton sayin', 'How's everythin' with the army these days?' So, says I to myself, he's got me spotted already. 'Don't ask me,' I toss back to him, 'I ain't botherin' 'bout no army these days.' 'You ain't quit?' he stabs at me, sharp-like. 'Yep,' says I. 'No more o' that business for me.' 'Why not?' he wants to know. An' I've got a sneakin' hunch he ain't believin' what I'm tellin' him. 'Well, for one thing,' says I, 'it's too long 'tween drinks.' 'You mean,' says he, 'it's too long 'tween pay days.' An' right then it looks to me like he's havin' a hard time keepin' from lickin' his chops when he's speakin' o' pay days. Anyways, I says to him, 'You're right as seven rabbits, feller.'

"Just then Jake Plummer busts in. 'Jake,' says I, 'you're the very feller I been lookin' for.' Next minute me an' Jake is sittin' at a table in a far corner.

'You're shore keepin' queer company these days,' Jake hands me first off. ' ever mind that,' says I. 'He shore ain't no friend o' mine. Thought was I still with. the army, I reckon, an' he'd do a little pumpin.'

" 'Well,' says Jake, full o' surprise 'ain't you in the army no more?' 'Nope,' says I, 'I've took up farmin', Jake. An' that's what I want to talk to you 'bout.' 'Farmin',' Jake 'most nigh shouts, lookin' at me sort o' queer-like. What you aimin' to do, starve to death?' 'Starvin',' says I, 'ain't no worse'n some other brands what's a heap more plentiful. Yep, I figure to give it a whirl, Jake. But I need help.' 'An' you know where you can get it, don't you?' Jake says to me.

"Well, to make a long story longer mebbe, me an' Jake make a deal. I tell him I need some feed right quick, an' there ain't none in Dogtown. Don't want much, some hay an' oats to keep my hoss an' cow goin' till the grass is up agin. On top o' that I'll need a team an' wagon to haul the stuff to Dogtown. Can't pay him now 'cause I'm busted. But he'll have my hoss, him bein' worth any six hosses in Jake's barn. An' I'll be back with the team an' the money quick as the next pay comes through. So it's all fixed, an' I have me a right peaceful sleep that night.

"Next day I don't do much 'cept load the wagon with twenty bales o' hay an' a couple o' sacks o' oats. I'm out in the barnyard loadin' up, when young Hilton comes by. 'Course, I don't let on I see him. But I'm mighty shore he seen what I was doin'. Now mebbe that buzzard's satisfied, I says to myself.

"It's after dark when the stage gets in that evenin'. They change hosses at Hartersville. I see Jake Plummer takin' the lead team to the barn so I shy up to the stage driver. Tm supposed to be ridin' to Dogtown with you tonight,' I tell him, an' hand him the order what the colonel had give me. 'Good 'nough,' says he. 'Where's the loot?' I ask him. 'Up on top,' says be, sort o' whisperin'. 'Couple o' bundles under them mail sacks.'

"Well, the passengers is gettin' themselves some grub next door to Jake's. An' the stage driver ain't long doin' the same. Now there's a mighty cold wind blowin' tonight, an' folks is keepin' indoors sort o' close. So I have me a look at the top o' that stage, just to make shore that feller ain't lied to me.

"After a while I take a peek at the Bighorn. There ain't a soul in the place, 'ceptin' the sleepy barkeep. Well, thinks I, it's too early to tum in, so I'll just take me a walk. Now, r reckon I must've walked a couple o' hours, or more. Anyways, when I get back to the village, I see the stage has pulled out. Yep,. I'd shore missed it, but somehow or other it didn't seem to worry me none. I just slip back to Ma Plummer's an' hit the hay, sleepin' like a bear in midwinter.

" 'Say, feller,' says Jake next mornin', 'where was you last night? Curley was shore in a stew. Claimed you was 'sposed to be ridin' back with him.' 'Curley's coo-coo,' says I, goin' after my bosses.

"Well, it ain't long 'fore I'm on my way to Dogtown. An' I'm tellin' you, folks, I shore ain't unhappy neither. I'm whistlin' *Turkey in the Straw,* an' just 'bout as contented as a polecat in a graveyard. I take it easy, an' it's gettin' 'long toward sundown when I pull into camp agin. Figure I better stop off an' sort o' report my intentions to the colonel.

"An' one o' the first fellers I see is the colonel himself, 'Howdy, Colonel,' says I, pleasant as a bunch o' onions. But there ain't no answer. The colonel, he just stares at me, an' the longer he stares, the hotter I can see he's gettin'. After a while he gets hold o' his tongue. 'Dawson,' he barks at me, 'why wasn't you on the stage last night?' Well, I'll tell you, Colonel,' says I. 'I ain't so fond o' stage ridin'. It's too confinin'. I'm a heap more comfortable ridin' in the open.'

"Then the colonel barks agin. But this time he's callin' the sergeant o' the guard. 'Sergeant,' says he, 'put this man under arrest.' '"What you 'restin' me for, Colonel?' I ask him.

'What for!' he shouts back at me. 'Just so I'll be shore you appear at a court martial in the mornin'.'

" 'Court martial!' says I, unbelievin' like. 'What's the charge?' 'Charges, not charge,' he snaps back. 'Willful dis-obedience, an' insubordination. An' we might as well add robbery to it. The stage comes in last night, an' you ain't on it. Neither is the money. It was held up in Buffalo Gulch, but the bandits didn't find nothin'. Explain that to the court) if you can. Lock him up, Sergeant.'

" 'Now wait a minute, Colonel,' says I. 'There ought to be a easier way out o' this than callin' a court martial. Let's see if we can find it.' Now, I'm back in the wagon by this time, pokin' into one o' them sacks o' oats. I pull somethin' out, an' hand it to the colonel. 'You reckon that's what you was lookin' for?' I ask him.

"Well, the colonel looks at me like I'm somethin' he can't find no name for. Then he grins, an' says to me, 'Dawson, you only obeyed half the order I give you. You saved the money all right, but you let Copper Hilton get away. I've a mind to court martial you, anyways.' "

"Did the colonel carry out his threat?" someone asked.

"Nope," Jim replied, with a grin, "he just put me on double rations for a full week."

# Perfect Contentment

THE DUDES HAD RIDDEN TO the head of Big Canyon this morning. They were now grouped against one of the granite wall , resting in a narrow strip of shade before the return trip. Two buzzards circled lazily overhead. A tiny stream slipped silently over the smooth rocks almost at their feet, only to disappear in the sand a short distance away.

"What a peaceful spot!" a recent arrival remarked, with a sigh.

"Yes, peaceful beyond imagination," came from another guest. "And that reminds me. Jim, in your story about the bandits you used a phrase I had never heard before. It has puzzled me considerably. Speaking of your return to camp with your load of hay and oats, you said you were as contented as a skunk in a graveyard. Now what I want to know is, why that animal should be able to find contentment in a cemetery?"

Jim Dawson was rolling a cigarette, and before he could offer an explanation another of the party spoke up. "Yes, I wondered about that myself. Of all places in the world, I would think a cemetery would be the last to offer contentment for anything."

"Oh, I dunno," Jim drawled, as he lit the cigarette. "I ain't never heard o' the folks what has to stay in them places complainin' 'bout it. They shore seem contented 'nough."

"But that isn't answering the question, Jim," the dude laughingly responded.

"Well, it's like this," Jim explained. "Everybody knows a polecat is a

Perfect Contentment

mighty unpopular animal. Seems like he ain't never learned how to get 'long with folks. Now Mister Polecat knows that. It ain't no secret to him, where he stands with humans. He's a outcast from society, you might say, an' he knows it mighty well.

"An' he's smart 'nough to know somethin' else too. He knows there ain't no safer place in the world than a graveyard. So, you see, he's got a right to be contented. He knows mighty well dead folks ain't feared o' him, an' so they ain't apt to be botherin' him."

# Gift from the Clouds

*J*IM DAWSON HAD BEEN TELLING
a story of the early days in the West, the days when he rode the range. "Jim," one of his friends remarked, when the story had been finished, "a cowboy's life must have been frightfully lonely in those days."

"Oh, no," Jim replied, appraising a cigarette he had just rolled. "Leastwise, I never thought on it as bein' 'specially lonesome."

"I don't see how it could have been otherwise."

"Well, mebbe that was 'cause I never bothered thinkin' 'bout it," Jim offered.

"But how could you help thinking about it?" one of the women wanted to know. "You'll never convince me that you were not lonely. Especially at night, far from home and no one to talk with."

"Well, I might be a right smart way from home, Miss," Jim drawled, "but I shore wasn't alone. You see, my hoss wasn't never far off, an' I could talk to him when I wanted to. 'Course, I don't reckon any o' you folks ever talked to a hoss. An' if he looked like he wasn't interested, I could generally stir up a one-way argument with myself. Yep, there was always company. I could hear the coyotes barkin'. An' all kinds o' bugs chatterin' 'bout their affairs. Nope, I wasn't never lonesome."

"I still think it was a rough and lonesome life," Jim's friend persisted.

"Oh, it might've been a mite rough. But there was always somethn' mighty good waitin' for a feller."

"That was pay day; I suppose."

"Nope, I never give much thought to pay day. If the boss had said to me, 'Jim, which would you rather have, a tub o' hot water an' a good meal, or this here paycheck? Take your choice; I reckon I'd said to him, 'Thanks, boss, you can keep that piece o' paper.'

"Nope, just bein' home for a spell was 'nough for me. Money didn't look so important. "When I'd get some good grub under my belt I wouldn't trade hats with the King o' England. 'Course, that poor feller never had a chance at real livin'.

"You see, it's like this," Jim continued. "Folks what's always had every-thin' ain't apt to be apprecatin' 'em so well. Now I don't reckon any o' you folks has ever seen the time when you didn't have all the water you wanted. It ain't likely you ever pulled a blanket over you at night when you was plastered with dust an' sweat. Then startin' another day with scarce 'nough water to make you a can o' coffee.

'I'm tellin' you, after you've took that for a while you're most likely to get a mighty tender feelin' for that gift from the clouds what ain't too plentiful in these parts. An' you ain't likely to be takin' your blessin' for granted. When you're home agin, an' got yourself a good scrubbin', you feel sort o' like you've been turned inside out, an' made all over agin."

# In the Long, Long Ago

JIM DAWSON HAD TAKEN THE dudes into Tomahawk Canyon this morning. They were now resting in the shade before the return trip. Naturally, the first question was. "Dawson, how did this place get its name?"

"Dunno," Jim replied, scratching an ear, " 'less it was 'count o' what the white men found when they first come into this country. Folks claims tomahawks was so thick there wasn't scarce room for grass to grow. There must've been a big battle up here."

"Did you ever find any tomahawks, Jim?"

"Nope, they was all gone long 'fore I moved in."

"It must have been quite a problem for the Indians to get around before they had horses," someone remarked.

"Oh, they didn't have no trouble gettin' 'round in the ol' days," Jim drawled. "Fact is, they could travel a heap faster than they did after the hoss come 'long."

"How could that be?"

"Well, you see, snappin' turtles was plentiful them days. Now snappin' turtles is right friendly sort o' critters, if a feller knows how to handle 'em. Leastwise they started out that way. An' the Injuns always aimed to keep a few o' them fellers handy. When they wanted to go someplace, all they had to do was hop on one o' them turtles."

It so happened that one of the guests was a university professor from the East. He was visiting Rainbow for the first time, hence he was not acquainted with Jim Dawson. He now expressed himself. "That would make a right good story for small children," he remarked. "But you surely don't expect adults to accept it."

"Why not, Professor?" Jim asked, as he lit a fresh cigarette.

'For two very simple reasons. First, the turtle is not of sufficient size."

"Right you are," Jim interrupted. "He shore ain't big 'nough these days. But way back in early times he was a heap bigger. Yep, ten times – mebbe a hundred times bigger'n he is now." The professor smiled.

"Even so," he said, "the turtle was not constructed for the purpose you speak of. His legs are far too small for either speed, or lengthy travel."

"But, you see," was Jim's smiling response, "Mister Turtle wasn't dependin' on his legs them days."

"By what other means could he navigate?" the professor asked, in a somewhat irritated tone.

"He flew," was Jim's calm reply.

"Flew!"

"Yep. Mister Turtle had powerful wings them days." Even the professor was forced to join in the laughter.

"Well, what's the catch?" he asked.

"Ain't no catch to it. Leastwise not so far as I know."

"Then what became of their wings?" the professor inquired. Jim shifted his position, which generally indicated a lengthy story in prospect.

"Well," he began, "it seems it was somethin' like this. Now I wasn't there, 'course, so I ain't vouchln' for it. I got the story from ol' Foxear, an' he swears it's straight. Now he claims the turtle clan has a convention up near Salt Lake. 'Cordin' to Foxy, they only held conventions onct in a hundred years. An' any self-respectin' turtle would've chewed off his hind legs rather'n miss it.

"Now, Foxy says this was the biggest meetin' what the turtles had ever pulled off. They come in from all over the land, an' it lasted for 'most nigh a month. When the powwow is over, one o' the chiefs suggests they all fly over to the lake, an' have 'em a swim. Now this swimmin' in salt water is somethin' new for them turtles, an' they have such a big time they stay in the water most o' the day." At this point Jim found it necessary to roll another cigarette, while the dudes waited impatiently.

'Well," he finally continued, "when them fellers come out o' the water, their wings is so heavy they can't fly. An' 'fore they can figure out what to do 'bout it, that salt begins to dry. It just pastes their wings to their backs. They roll on the sand, an' the sand sticks to the salt. An' when nighttime comes they're packin' a roof over 'em. So there ain't nothin' to do but start walkin'. Now, they ain't used to much walkin', so I reckon a lot o' them snappers never got home. An' carryin' so much weight might've stunted their growth. Mebbe that's why a turtle's disposition ain't quite as good as it was in the early days. Anyways, they was never knowed to grow wings agin."

# Somewhat Undesirable

"**I**S THAT AN INDIAN BELT you're wearing, Mr. Dawson?" A newcomer to Rainbow had put the question to Jim one day.

"That's right, Miss," Jim replied.

"What an odd design. The one on the buckle, I mean. Is it supposed to represent something?"

"Yep, it shore is. That's a hunch-bug, Miss."

"A hunch-bug?"

"Yep. An' a three-legged one, too. Ain't you never heard o' hunch-bugs?"

"I certainly never have."

"Now, ain't that too bad," Jim drawled. "Thought most everybody knowed 'bout hunch-bugs. Just 'bout the most interestin' bugs I knows on."

"Tell us about them, Jim," one of his friends requested. Jim rolled a cigarette with the usual deliberation.

"Oh, there ain't a lot to tell about 'em," he finally said. "They're mighty well liked by the Injuns, 'cause they don't eat nothin' but ants."

"How does that make them so popular with the Indians?" someone asked.

"Well, you can see for yourselves how it would be," Jim returned, as he scratched an ear. "You come home in the evenin', an' find the ants has been callin' on you. An' they've packed off that corn meal you figured on havin' for supper. Sooo – the Injuns just keep a few hunch-bugs on hand to take care o' the ants when they come callin'."

"But," the first dude asked, "you spoke of the one on that buckle as having only three legs. How many should they have?"

"Well," Jim replied, "most generally they pack four legs. But them with three legs is special"

"Special in what way?"

"You might call 'em weather prophets, I reckon." The dudes waited while Jim took time to roll a cigarette. "The Injuns," Jim finally explained, "aim to keep one o' them three-legged fellers 'round to sort o' keep 'em posted on the weather. You see, hunch-bugs is naturally black, but when a storm's brewin', them three-legged fellers get sort o' grayish

lookin'. When it's goin' to snow, they turn most nigh white."

"How interesting," someone remarked. "Where can these insects be found?"

"Well, they most generally hang 'round damp places, if they can find one. But they're gettin' mighty scarce these days, since rain's got to be most nigh as scarce as snakes' ears.

Foxear claims they was right plentiful back in the ol' days."

"I would certainly like to find one," came from another dude.

"Well," Jim returned, "the next time ol' Foxy comes 'long I'll tell him to pick me up one. But it ain't goin' to be one o' them three-legged critters."

"Why not? I would think that would be the most desirable one to have."

"Nope, not for me. Now, generally speakin', they ain't a bad lot. But when they get ready to push in the last o' their chips, they – well, they just ain't the same breed o' cats. You see, they get sort o' unhappy when they find out their number's up. Ol' Foxy, he claims it takes 'em three days gettin' ready to die. The first day they eat one o' their hind legs, next day they eat the other. An' on the third day they eat that foreleg o' theirs. Then's when a feller shore better be makin' tracks." Jim snuffed his cigarette, as though that was the end of the day's entertainment.

"Now, wait a minute, Jim," one of the dudes demanded. "Just what do you mean by 'making tracks'?"

"Well," came the drawling reply, "Foxy says when Mister Bug gets his legs all chewed up, he's meaner'n a rattlesnake. Seems like his own meat don't agree with him, an' he swells up like a poisoned pup. Then that crazy bug starts squirtin' poison all over the place."

"Oh, horrible!" exclaimed the dude whose innocent remark had started this tale.

"Yep, it shore is, Miss," Jim smilingly agreed. "An' Foxy claims them crazy critters can spit over as big a haystack as you ever seen."

# The Sunflower Omelet

*I*T WAS MIDSUMMER, AND THE heat was oppressive. A refreshing breeze had swept through the valley in whispering waves during the night. Now, however, the morning was well spent and, contrary to custom, the breeze had failed to return on its northward journey.

The guests at Rainbow had agreed that it was even too hot to ride. A keen observer might have seen that there was one who had accepted that decision with reluctance. A frown clouded her bright and eager face, but she said nothing. Her eyes were upon the disappearing form of Jim Dawson. Slowly, the frown also disappeared, and she was smiling as she quietly left her fellow guests in the shade of the friendly trees.

This young person from the far East was no stranger to Rainbow Ranch. Her time in this land of enchantment was definitely limited, and she was in no mood to waste a minute of it. An intriguing thought had flashed through her active mind, followed by instant action. She was now following Jim Dawson, as he made his way toward the corral.

"Jim," she said, when she had caught up with him, "you don't think it's too hot to ride, do you?"

"Hot?" Jim smilingly replied. "Why, this ain't a hot day. Reckon the folks is just sort o' lazy this mornin'. Most likely they'll be minded to ride when the sun goes down."

"They probably will," was the gloomy response. Then, after a moment's silence, "But I don't want to wait that long. Couldn't you and I ride this morning?"

"Shore," was the hearty reply. "I'll put you on Lady, an' let you be the guide. You can go wherever you've a mind to."

"Oh, grand!" she exclaimed, clapping her hands in glee. "But it's rather late for much of a ride. I wonder if we could –"

"Could what?"

"Never mind. It was something I thought would be nice, but it would probably be asking too much."

"Ain't never heard o' nobody ever bein' strung up for askin'," Jim drawled. "What was you thinkin' on, a slice o' the moon for lunch?"

"Yes," she laughingly returned, "I was thinking of lunch. But I would not care for anything as cold as the moon. I was only thinking how nice it would be to have lunch up in the hills. Then we could have a long ride afterward. Do you think we could get the cook to fix us something?"

"No need botherin' the cook," was Jim's prompt reply. "You tell the Lady Boss what we're up to, an' I'll rustle the makin's."

It was considerably past the noon hour when they found a cool spot far up Big Canyon. In a matter of minutes, Jim had a small fire underway. "What's the menu, Jim?" the fair guest inquired, as she curiously watched the unpacking of saddlebags.

"Oh, the usual layout," Jim drawled, as he placed a skillet over the fire. "There's always fresh eggs in the henhouse, you know. So all I had to snitch when the cook wasn't lookin' was a hunk o' bacon, an' a couple o' potatoes. Reckon that'll hold you till suppertime?"

"It will, indeed," was the eager response. "But I have a favor to ask of you, Jim."

She was not disturbed, however, by the stern voice which answered, "Again. What flavor is it this time?"

"I – " She hesitated an instant. "I want to do the cooking."

"Humpf! Don't think much of my cookin', I see. Well –" "Of course, I do," she interrupted. "But I'm curious. I've never done any cooking. But

I've watched you, and I want to try it for myself, May I?"

"Why, shore," was Jim's grinning reply. "Take off your shoes an' wade in. You have my best wishes."

"But I don't want you watching me."

"Adios," Jim returned, as he started down the canyon. "Whistle when it's ready," he called back.

Jim Dawson was long experienced in preparing a quick meal in the open. And the product which came from that one skillet always brought forth generous approval from the dudes. This ambitious young person had often watched Jim prepare such a meal. She had failed, however, to observe the efficiency of his method. Bacon was first on the skillet, followed by potatoes, and by the time coffee was ready, the eggs had been scrambled to a turn. But with the new cook, all three ingredients had been tossed onto the skillet at the same time.

It was a decidedly troubled voice which Jim heard calling him a short while later. But even that had failed to prepare him for the picture of utter dejection which met his eyes. His fair companion was sitting close to the dying fire with her face in her hands.

"What's wrong?" Jim asked, as he came up beside her.

"Everything," was the plaintive reply. "Look at that," and she took the lid off the skillet. "Who could eat such a horrid-looking mess?"

Jim looked. A smile slowly spread over his bronzed features, then quickly vanished. He had always enjoyed teasing this high-spirited girl, but this was no time for flippancy. He laid a hand gently on the bowed head. when he spoke, there was an unaccustomed gentleness in his voice.

"Why, you an' I can eat it, honey. Mebbe it don't look too pretty, but looks shore ain't everythin'. If they was, Jim Dawson would be in a bad way."

"It looks like something the cat might have dragged out of the wash," she groaned, looking up with tear-dimmed eyes.

"Nope, can't agree with you," Jim returned. "I'll tell you what it looks like to me. It looks like a sunflower." She dashed the tears from her eyes, as though to see if he were only joking. What she saw was a kindly smile, and she heard, "Yep, it looks like a sunflower what's been through a hailstorm. 'But it ain't really hurt none. It's the same flower. It ain't lost nothin', 'ceptin' its beauty. An' Jim Dawson shore ain't pickin' on good looks to satisfy his appetite."

# Speaking of Nuts

*J*IM DAWSON WAS HAVING TROUble with the old guitar this evening. Therefore, Doctor Jimmie filled the interlude with one of his favorite stories.

"It was about four o'clock," he began, "when my last patient left the office. I went to the window to look out upon one of the worst storms I could remember. The wind was howling, and the rain was coming down in sheets. Not a human being was to be seen.

"I was still standing there when my wife came into the room. She glanced out the window rather indifferently, then looked up at me. 'Jimmie,' she said, 'why don't you lie down and rest for a while? No one will be coming in until this storm is over. And you look so tired.'

"I *was* tired, for I had been out most of the night be ore. 'For once,' I told her, 'I think I'll take your advice. No one but a nut would be abroad in this weather.' The bell rang as I started to my room. Mary opened the door, and I saw a man standing there with water streaming from his hat. He was a stranger. He spoke rather timidly. 'McNutt is my name;' he said. 'I was – ' But Mary interrupted him.

" 'Yes, of course,' she said. 'Come in, Mr. Nutt, the doctor was expecting you'."

"Now it's your turn, Jim," someone suggested, when quiet was restored.

"Well," Jim returned, "I shore ain't got none to match that one. Doc Jimmie's got me backed off the trail when it comes to fresh handmade yams."

"We admire your modesty, Jim," was the doctor's prompt response, "but I'm quite certain your stories are not all shopworn."

Jim scratched an ear before replying. "Well," he said, as he laid the guitar aside, "I might give you one concernin' a doctor who thought I was a nut, I reckon. It was like this.

"It was the last year I was with the Lazy R. The boss sends me to town to meet some folks what was comin' in on the evenin' train. Findin' the train's 'bout three hours late, I figure to look up a ol' friend o' mine.

"This feller's name was Banker, but he shore didn't live up to the name when I knowed him. 'Cept on pay day, he never had nothin' what looked like money. An' Red's shore ol' 'nough to know better when he gets married all o' a sudden. I ain't s en him since he's been tied, an' that's quite a spell now.

"I'd heard as how he'd quit his job, an' was livin' in town. An' bein' sort o' curious concernin' my ol' friend, I go call on him. It was Red himself opened the door, an' 1 was shore took back. Might've passed him up, if I'd seen him on the street. He was shore decorated.

"Well, I sort o' chuckle to myself when I slide into a big leather chair. It shore don't take no brains to figure it out. Red must've had a good look at the gal's purse 'fore he roped'. her. An' he seen she was packin' somethin' a heap more useful than her war paint.

" 'Well, Red,' says I, 'how goes it these days?'

" 'Not so good, right now,' says Red. 'Wife's sick. Expectin' a baby any minute.' Then I hear somebody yippin' upstairs. 'Make yourself at home,' says Red. 'I'll see what the wife wants. That fool doctor should been here 'fore now.'

"Well, Red ain't gone more'n a couple o' minutes when the doorbell rings, an' I hear him yellin', 'You go to the door, Jim, I'm busy.' Now, when I open the door I'm lookin' at a feller I ain't never seen. 'Howdy,' says I. He looks me over sort o' queer-like, then he says, 'My name's Crane. I'm the —'

"But I cut him off sharp. 'Well, stranger,' says I, 'reckon you've got the wrong house. The folks here is lookin' for a feller, but his name ain't Crane. It's Stork'.'"

# No Ordinary Affair

"JIM, I'VE HEARD YOU TELL about leaving home at a very early age. But I don't believe you ever told us why that was." That had come from one of Jim Dawson's good friends one day. "Was there some trouble at home?"

"Nope," Jim replied, gazing off into the distance. "Nope, we never had no trouble at home. That is, nothin' what a feller might call serious. There was a couple o' reasons for my leavin'. First off, if was a big family, an' Dad wasn't havin' it too easy. I figure if some of us get out, the load ain't apt to be so heavy. Top o' that, it looked like a right good way o' settlin' a difference o' opinion concernin' yours truly.

"You see," he continued, after a thoughtful pause, "I was sort o' set on bein' a cowpoke. But Dad was agin it, sayin' there wasn't no future in it – an' I reckon he was right. He wanted I should be a blacksmith. Now, I'd been a carpenter, if Granddad could've had his way. An' Ma, she was an for havin' me a preacher. Now, there I was, bein' pulled to pieces by them well-meanin' folks. An' seein' as how I can't please 'em all, I figure mebbe I'd do 'bout as well tryin.' to please Jim Dawson."

"How many children were there?" his friend asked. "Nine."

"Are many of them still living?"

"Mebbe a couple o' the younger ones. I ain't shore." "Don't you ever write to them?"

"Nope. Writin' letters ain't in my line."

"Did you ever go back to your home?" another dude wanted to know.

"Onct," Jim replied, as he gazed thoughtfully at a fresh cigarette. "Heard one o' my kid sisters was gettin' married. Got sort o' curious to see what she'd roped. Reckon she was married all right, but you couldn't prove it by me."

"You were too late for the wedding, I suppose."

"Nope. Looked sort o' like 1 was too early. You see, the folks was busy gettin' ready for the big doin's. Mother an' Dad was glad to see me, 'course. But the others – well, it looked like they hardly knowed who I was. But I'd been gone from home for quite a spell, so you couldn't scarce blame 'em, I reckon. Anyways, I'm in the kitchen scraping some o' the dust off me when Sis comes in. She looks me over like I might be a peddler, an' says, 'Say, you ain't goin' to the weddin' lookin' like that?' 'Why not?' says I. 'What's wrong with my looks?' 'Ain't you got no necktie?' she wants to know.

"Well, I bust out laughin', which might've been a mistake. Anyways, it shore didn't help none. 'Now, what in Noah's name would I be wantin' with one o' them things?' says I. 'I've got most nigh as much use for a neck-strangler as a pig has for two tails.' 'Well,' says she, 'when you go to town you better get yourself one, an' wear it, too. This ain't no hillbilly weddin'.'

"Now when I last seen Sis, she was wearin' pigtails, but she'd growed to be a right smart-lookin' filly by this time. But you see, folks, she'd been 'way to school, an' it seemed like she'd took on more airs than larnin'. Anyways, home wasn't good 'nough for her weddin'. Nope she's havin' herself a church weddin', with all the trimmin's. Well, I go to town all right, but I don't stop off for the weddin'. An' that was my last home-goin'."

# Book Larnin'

HE FOLLOWING MORNING, JIM guided his party into Panther Gulch. Near the head of that picturesque, if somewhat awesome gorge, he halted. Horses and riders alike appeared grateful for the opportunity to rest before the return trip.

"Jim, I've been thinking about what you told us yesterday concerning your one and only visit to your old home." One of the dudes had thus opened the conversation. "From your remarks, I gathered that you don't have a very high regard for higher education." Jim was slow in responding.

"Me?" he finally drawled, as he scratched an ear. "Nope, I ain't got nothin' agin it."

It was evident to those who knew him that here was a subject which was of no interest to Jim Dawson. There were present, however, several who had known him but a few days. Therefore, the subject was discussed at some length, while Jim silently tossed pebbles into the tiny stream which gurgled over the rocks nearby.

"Jim," someone finally asked, "if you had children, wouldn't you want them to have a college education?" Jim smiled. The dudes rarely missed an opportunity to put him on the spot.

"Well," he slowly replied, "I reckon any kids o' mine would be too busy rustlin' their keep, same as the ol' man."

"But suppose you were able to send them to college," the dud persisted. "Wouldn't you want them to have that advantage?"

"Advantage?" Jim repeated, scratching an ear. "Now I ain't shore 'bout that."

"What do you mean?"

"Well, seein' as how I ain't had no education, mebbe I'd better be keepin' my notions to myself."

"Not at all," was the prompt return. "I'm sure we would all be glad to have your opinion."

"Oh, it don't 'mount to nothin'," Jim drawled. "But figurin' on what my eyes an' ears has took in, it looks to me like this educatin' business is sort o' like a dose o' caster oil. Some can take it, an' some can't."

When the laughter had subsided, Jim was pressed for an explanation. He kept bis audience in suspense, however, while he rolled a fresh cigarette.

"Well, speakin' to an' fro, as Dad used to say, it looks somethin' like this to me. Time them colleges get through stuffin' a youngster's head with book larnin' there ain't apt to be much room left for a bit o' hoss-sense." With that Jim rose, and stretched himself. "Come on folks, it's time we was shovin' off."

"But, Jim," someone protested, "you're not being fair –" "Mebbe not," Jim interrupted, "but you can shore lay a safe bet on one thing. Jim Dawson's opinions ain't apt to make no change in the price o' eggs."

Worthy of Acquaintance

"OH, WHAT A RELIEF," sighed the fair one, as she sank to the ground. Jim Dawson had taken the dudes into Big Canyon today. "There's one thing about this country that 1 certainly do not like," she announced.

"What's that, Miss?" Jim asked, taking his usual seat on his bootheels.

"That awful wind."

"Oh, you'd likely get used to that," was the smiling reply. "Wind ain't bad when you get 'quainted with it. It's a part o' Nature, you know. An' I figure it ain't smart to be quarrelin' with Nature. We'd shore know what trouble was if we didn't have the sun, the rain an' the wind."

"Sun and rain are fine," she admitted, "but I could certainly get along without the wind."

"Yep, I can see how you feel 'bout it," Jim returned. "Reckon it's the same way concernin' some o' the folks we know. One o' 'em happens to be a big talker, an' we wonder how come he has so many friends. Well, his friends know he's a big-hearted feller, an' does a heap o' good mebbe we don't know 'bout. He's too windy to suit us, so we just don't like him."

"You're indeed charitable," the dude responded, "but that doesn't change my opinion of the wind. You haven't shown me any good in it."

"Well, I reckon that's 'cause you ain't got 'quainted with Mister Wind. Now, it ain't likely we'd be out here, if he wasn't on the job." "Why not?"

" 'Cause it. would more'n likely be too hot to move. Yep, Mister Wind can be mighty good to us sometimes. Trouble is, we ain't minded to give him credit for it. I hear folks cussin' him when he blows their hats off, or puffs dust in their eyes. Shore, he plays tricks on us now an' agin, but I reckon he's got a right to a bit o' fun 'long the way. A happy-go-lucky feller, Mister Wind is. Comes an' goes when he pleases. Sings while he works, an' he shore ain't askin' favors o' nobody."

The group was thoughtfully silent, while Jim gazed up at a hawk drifting contentedly on the breeze. "There was a time when I didn't think much o' Mister Wind neither," he resumed. "But that was 'fore I got to know him.

Did me a good turn onct, an' I ain't forgot it."

"What was that, Jim?" someone asked, when he failed to elucidate.

"Well, this was 'way back in the early days. I'd got sort o' tired wanderin'. Got a notion I'd like to get a place o my own, an' settle down. So I get me a parcel o' land, an' a few cows for a starter. Then I build me a cabin. Now I'm gettin' 'long fine till I come to the roofin'. I'm up on the roof feelin' right merry-like one mornin'. That's 'cause I figure to have that job done by sundown. Get the first roll o' roofin' tacked down when I feel a gnawin' under my belt.

"Now I ain't needin' no doctor to tell me how to cure such a ailment. I can see by the sun as how it ain't quite noontime. But I ain't never been much for follerin' a timetable. So I get me in the shade not far off, m have me some lunch. There's a friendly breeze singin' through the treetops. It's mighty comfortable there, so I don't hurry myself none.

"After a while, I notice the breeze is getting right frisky by spells. I ain't concernin' myself 'bout it; that is, not till I got back to work. That strip o' roofin' I'd just put on wasn't no place in sight. It had went with the wind while I'd been enjoyin' myself.

"Now, I was hoppin' mad for a minute or so. Was 'bout to do some fancy cussin' – an' I was right good at it them days – when somethin' pops into my empty head. So I sit down on a nail keg, an' let the thing settle. I'm rollin' me a cigarette when it finally jells – or words o' that meanin'. Yep, it's plain as a pimple on a feller's nose. Mister Wind had done me a fa or. An' I shore thanked him for it right then an' there.

"You see, I'd heard as how this was a bad place for hailstorms, but hadn't paid no heed to it. Mister Wind felt sort o' sorry for me I reckon. He knowed I had no business puttin' paper on that roof. Most likely it wouldn't lasted through the winter. Well, I pack the rest o' that roofin' paper to town, an' get me some shingles. An' I was shore grateful to Mister Wind for his kindly interest in me."

Probably the subject would have been dropped, had one of the dudes not remarked, "I admire your philosophy, Jim. But how do you account for the wind doing so much damage at times?"

"Don't bother tryin'," was the reply. "Reckon there's some good reason, but I shore ain't smart 'nough to figure it out."

"Does the wind cause you much trouble here?" someone asked.

"Nope. That is, nothin' too serious. Gets a bit frisky now an' agin, but we don't mind it. Like the time it walked off with the hayshed – but I forgot – that wasn't here. That was up north, the first summer I was with the Lazy R. I ain't never seen the wind quite so frisky down here."

"Tell us about the hayshed, Jim."

"Well, we didn't have a very big barn then. It was hayin' time, an' we had the barn full. But there was a tall hayshed standin' on four stout legs.

"We were all set to fill up the shed when the wind comes up out o' the south. It gets to friskin' so we have to quit workin'. By sundown, that wind was shore travelin'. An' when we crawl out next mornin', we find we ain't got no hayshed. It had went with the wind. It hadn't left no word regardin' where it might be goin', so we didn't bother lookin' for it.

"Well, that evenin' one o' the boys come in, sayin' he seen the shed out by Big Mesa. So me an' the boss goes out next mornin' to hav us a look. An' shore 'nough, there was that hayshed leanin' agin the rock just as contented as a mouse in a featherbed.

"The boss looks it over, an' says to me, 'It ain't hurt none, Jim. So we'll go back an' get the wagon an' some tools. You can tear it down, an' rebuild it in a couple o' days.'

"Now by the time we get back to the ranch that wind is rippin' down out o' the north. Must've been the same one what went up the day before. Anyways, the boss says, 'Reckon you better let that job go till this wind sobers up some.' 'Course that ain't nowise disappointin' to me. Shore, I could do the job all right, but I knowed a lot o' things I'd be more pleased 'bout. But I never had to rebuild that shed." Jim felt in need of a fresh smoke at this point.

"Why not?" an impatient dude asked.

"Well," he finally concluded, "I figure Mister Wind had got sort o' absent-minded on his way north. He forgot I was a friend o' his when he walked off with that hayshed. Now, he ain't aimin' to cause me a lot o' trouble, so he comes back to sort o' square himself. First thing I see next mornin' is that shed out by the barn.

"Yep, it was standing out there big as life. Looked like it was right pleased at bein' back home agin. An' ol' Mister Wind had set that hayshed down not more'n 'bout ten feet from where he'd picked it up.'

# In the Gloaming

$\mathcal{T}$HE RANCH HOUSE WAS UNUSU-
ally quiet this evening. The air was chilly, for summer had taken a sudden
departure. Even the new moon looked frosty as it slowly vanished behind
Black Mountain. The guests at Rainbow had also departed. Regardless
of the chill, however, Gipsy Lynn had taken her place on the veranda,
with the faithful Mike at her side. Dreamily, she watched the horses
frolicking down in the meadow. It was not long until Jim Dawson took
his usual seat on the steps, and leisurely rolled a cigarette.

Jim seldom volunteered any conversation, so it was Gipsy who broke a
rather prolonged silence. "Jim, I've known you for quite a while now, and
I must admit that I am still somewhat puzzled."

"Puzzled about what?" Jim asked, sending a smoke-ring into the still air.

"You."

"Me!" Jim laughed. "Shore don't know what anybody could find puzzlin'
'bout me – 'specially you. 'Course, I know my lingo ain't too easy to figure
out sometimes."

"No, it's not your lingo, as you choose to call it. I can understand your
speech without any difficulty. What amazes me is the way you manage
to handle various delicate situations that come up from time to time. If
you appear unable, or unwilling to give a direct answer to the many odd
questions that the guests put to you, you can usually manage a diplomatic
escape. I've had many a good laugh as I recalled your skill along that line.
At least a dozen times I've seen the folks do their best to extract the truth

concerning your age, but none have yet succeeded." Jim's only response was a low chuckle, as he gazed up at the stars.

"Perhaps you have known mote years than you enjoy counting," Gipsy continued. "But that doesn't mean that you are old. Age is not a matter of years. It is the spirit within us that determines age, and none can deny that your spirit is still youthful. I wonder why you insist on keeping your age a secret. Is it just because you enjoy tantalizing the, curious, or because you have some valid reason for keeping it to yourself?"

Jim was slow in answering. "Well," he finally said, "this is the way it looks to me. Now, you wouldn't ask your best friend how much money he had in the bank, would you? Shore you wouldn't, an' it's 'bout the same regardin' a feller's age. It looks to me like it ain't nobody's business how many years he's 'cumulated. His past is his treasure, an' if he has a mind to bury it, I reckon that's his affair."

Gipsy's laughter mingled with the shrill call of a coyote across the valley. "And I could certainly not take issue with your point of view," she remarked. "But your explanation only points up the fact that you can be decidedly blunt with your answers at times. I was somewhat concerned regarding your opinion of higher education, as you expressed it recently. I feared some of our highly cultured guests might have taken offense. I observed no evidence of it, however. But I didn't blame you. I thought it was quite unfair of them to put you on the spot the way they did. It looked too much as though they were trying to embarrass you. As usual, however, you got away with it. You have said you "had no schooling, yet you manage to hold your own quite well with those who have had considerable education. That is what puzzles me."

Jim rolled another cigarette. "Well, there ain't no way o' knowin', 'course, what education might've done to me. Anyways, it ain't likely it would've added much to my happiness. I reckon most o' what I know – an' that shore ain't much – has come from just watchin'. An' it's been mighty interestin', too."

"Watching the parade, so to speak?" Gipsy smilingly returned.

"Yep, I reckon that's a right good way o' puttin' it. You see, when I was just a saplin', my granddad told me some things I never forgot. One was that I could work my tongue overtime an' learn nothin', but not so with my eyes an' ears. 'Son,' he'd say to me, 'if you want to learn anythin' while you're stumblin' through this ol' world, be shore you make full use o' your eyes. They're 'bout the finest things the good Lord give us. Watch a dog, or a boss. Their sharp eyes never miss a thing what goes on 'round 'em. That's the way they learn.' Well, I started out with two right good eyes, an' I've tried to use 'em like the ol' boy told me. An' I reckon most o' what I've learned not to do has come from watchin' folks. While a big part o' what I found was worth imitatin' has come from animals."

# Knights of the Spur

*A* THREATENED RAILROAD strike was causing considerable uneasiness among the guests at Rainbow. They had been discussing the situation this afternoon, when someone asked:

"Jim, have the unions ever tried to organize the cowboys?"

"Unions?" Jim returned, inspecting a fresh cigarette. "Nope, not so far as I ever heard." Then his lazy eyes brightened, as he added. "Oh, shore, I most nigh forgot. A couple o' pinheads tried it onct. They wasn't representin' no union, though."

"What do you mean by 'pinheads'?"

"Oh, you know, the kind what don't pack much 'bove the ears. Them two hadn't never been on speakin' terms with work. Never knowed to hold a job more'n a couple o' weeks. Reckon they figured they'd be cuttin' themselves in on a soft deal, if they could round up 'nough saps."

Jim stretched his arms as though to dismiss the subject. He was not to be left off so easily, however. "Couldn't you tell us how it worked out?" someone asked.

"Oh, shore, but it ain't apt to be interestin'."

"We'll take a chance on that," was the prompt response. "Well," Jim began, "this wasn't long after I come into the north country. I was workin' for a outfit up in Wyomin' at the time. 'Course, I'd heard what them fellers was tryin' to cook up, but I hadn't met up with 'em. They claim they're goin' to put a stop to the slave labor v1hat the cowpokes had let themselves in for. 'When we're organized,' one dumbbell tells me, 'we'll be gettin' doable the regular pay, an' workin' no more'n ten hours a day.' Well, it shore sounds grand. But I don't notice no excitement 'mong the boys.

"Bein' in town one pay day, I drop into the Silver Star to see what might be stirrin'. Now 'cordin' to what I'd already picked up, them young missionaries hadn't been doin' so well. So they'd sent to Denver for help. Course, we didn't find out 'bout this hombre from Denver till the show was over. Smithers, he calls himself. Seems like he'd been treasurer for some union up there. But he was kicked out 'count o' his havin' sticky fingers. An' he shore looks like a slicker – shifty eye, an' a fishy handshake. Now he's down here helpin' to organize the cowpokes.

"Now, there ain't more'n half a dozen customers at the bar when I amble into the Silver Star. One is my ol' friend from Texas, Hank Summers. Hank has been up in this country for quite a spell. He knows everybody worth knowin', an' is mighty popular. He introduces me to Smithers. Smithers, he buys me a drink, an' I tuck it away to the gent's health.

"Then Smithers says to Hank, takin' up where he left off when I busted in, I reckon: 'Now, Summers,' says he, 'you'll have to admit this is a wonderful thing for the cowboys.'

" 'Yep,' says Hank, 'I reckon you're right – providin' you can put it over. But I've got fifty bucks what says you ain't got a chance.' 'Well,' says Smithers, 'I'd shore like to take that bet, but I ain't got the money right now.'

"Now, this Smithers, he's wearin' right fancy raiment, an' I see Hank squintin' at the feller's pants, sort o' queer-like. 'Well,' says Hank, 'if you're so all-fired shore o' yourself, I'll take them pants you're wearin', in place o' the fifty bucks.'

"The feller next to Hank laughs. 'We hadn't heard you was figurin' on gettin' spliced' says he. 'I ain't,' says Hank. 'I was thinkin' o' the parson. That poor devil hasn't had no decent rags since I've knowed him. The parson should look right smart in them pants. 'Bout his size too. What say, pardner?'

'Well, Smithers looks at his pants, sort o' sad-like for a minute. Then he says, 'Summers, I can shore use that fifty bucks. It's a bet.' An' they shake hands. You see, folks, them wasn't no run-o'-mine pants that hombre was wearin'. They was son o' dove-gray, with twisted black stripes. I hadn't never seen none like 'em before. An' I had to agree with Hank. They shore would perk up the poor ol' parson." Jim chuckled, as he snuffed his cigarette in the sand.

"After they shake hands, Smithers says, 'Now, seein' as you've staked your money agin it, I don't reckon there's any use o' me talkin' 'bout your comin' in with us.'

" 'Now, pardner,' says Hank, you got me all wrong. I ain't that kind. Nope, I wouldn't put so much as a toothpick in the way o' your success. Fact is, I might even help you win.' Smithers sort o' gasps. 'Help me!' says he. 'Shore,' says Hank, 'why not? You see it looks like I might be bettin' on a shore thing. That's 'cause o' me knowin' somethin' I don't reckon you've :run onto yet. Us cowpokes, pardner, is already organized'.'"

Jim began to roll another cigarette. Apparently that was the end of the story. But the dudes clearly indicated that they were not satisfied. "Come on, Jim, give us the rest of it," one .of his friends urged.

"Okay," Jim returned "but don't blame me when you're eatin' a cold supper. Now you see, folks, I don't know this Smithers ain't the only one what's workin' at this business. Hank Summers had been right busy, too. n' it turned out that Hank was a mighty good organizer.

'Well, I reckon I must've looked as much surprised as the feller from Denver when Hank says the cowpokes is already organized. I shore hadn't heard nothin' 'bout it. So I just stare at Hank, an' Smithers gulps his drink. 'How come I wasn't told 'bout this?' he wants to know, when he's located his tongue. "Cause,' Hank tells him, 'it's been a secret up to now.' 'What's the name o' this outfit?' Smithers asks.

'Knights o' the Spur,' says Hank. 'An' a mighty powerful outfit, if anybody be askin' you.'

"More'n likely my mouth's hangin' open by this time. Anyways, I hear Hank sayin', 'Now, I'm minded to make a deal with you, pardner.' 'What sort o' deal?' Smithers wants to know. 'Well,' says Hank, 'a mighty good one for you, I'd say – providin' we can put it over, 'course. Now I'm willin' to join up with your outfit, if you'll join the Knights o' the Spur.'

" 'You mean that?' Smithers shouts.

" 'Shore,' says Hank. 'Here's my hand on it. 'Course, I ain't guaranteein' nothin'. Don't know how the boys is apt to take it. But I'll do the best I can for you. Now, it just happens there's to be a meetin' o' the council tonight. An' if you'll be in here 'bout a hour after sundown, I'll put it up to 'em.'

"Now," Jim continued, with a grin, "it seems like I'm beginnin' to smell somethin' 'long 'bout this time. But I shore keep my trap shut. Anyways, I'm in the Silver Star long 'fore sundown that evenin'. Half a dozen o' the boys I know ease into the back room a while later. Then Hank comes in with Smithers. They're in that room for quite a spell. When they come out they're all lookin' right pleased with themselves. Hank hitches onto me, an' we all go over to Red Barker's livery barn.

"Now, there's a big lot back o' the barn, with a high board fence 'round it. That's where Red turns his hosses out to exercise when they ain't workin'. An' that's where the council is takin' Smithers for his 'nitiation." Jim's cigarette had gone out. He took his time relighting it, while the dudes waited impatiently.

"Well," he finally continued, "they blindfold the gent from Denver. Then somebody fetches a pot o' warm glue from the carpenter shop next door, an' they paint the feller's face. They do a fancy job, too. Then comes a sack o' goose feathers. They're blowed onto the glue. Reckon everybody's itchin' to laugh, but they don't. Nope, it's a mighty solemn business. That Smithers might o' looked a lot like Santa Claus, if he'd been fat 'nough.

"When the council had got Smithers' whiskers to suit 'em, somebody

Knights of the Spur

comes out o' the barn leadin' a mule. Right off, I see it's the Widder Jenkins' ol' mule, Noah. Ol' man Jenkins had been a prospector, an' Noah was 'bout all he left his widder when he turned in his chips. But she was mighty fond o' that ol' critter.

"Well, they put Smithers up on the mule, an' open the gate. 'Now, you blind seeker after truth,' says Hank Summers, 'you're commanded to ride this proud animal to the south end o' town, an' back agin. If you can do that without takin' off that blindfold, the council is willin' to accept you as a regular member o' the Knights o' the Spur.'

"Hank leads Noah out o' the gate, an' heads him south. Smithers is sittin' that mule like he' right proud o' himself. That is, till somebody empties a six-shooter. Poor ol' Noah, he tries to jump out o' his hide. I'm lookin' for Smithers to bite the dust, but he don't. He rips off the blindfold, an' hangs on somehow. Then somebody yells, 'Hoss-thief!' an' the sheriff pop out o' nowheres, an' takes a hand in the game.

"Well, the next thing we know the sheriff's draggin' Smithers up the courthouse steps. An' the crowd's yellin', 'String him up! Hang the boss-thief!' Then the judge busts through the crowd, an' climbs the steps. 'What's goin' on here?' he shouts to the sheriff. 'Plenty,' the sheriff growls. 'This coyote was tryin' to get away with Widder Jenkins' mule. An' I'm tryin' to save him from roostin' in one o' them trees.'

" 'Now, men,' the judge shouts, 'we want no hangin' here. We'll handle this case in a respectable legal way.' Well, they still claim that was the shortest trial on record. The room shore is crowded when the judge raps for order in the court. The sheriff makes his charge, an' Smithers tells his story. Now, that story he tells is shore 'nough straight, but there ain't nobody minded to believe it, 'course. An' the witnesses all bein' agin him, the gent from Denver don't have the chance o' a snowball in a bakeshop.

" 'James Smithers,' says the judge, 'the court finds you guilty o' the crime as charged. You're facin' two years, an' a fine o' a thousand dollars.

But this court o' justice bein' fair-minded, I'm givin' you a choice.'

'Well, Judge,' says Smithers, 'I'm shore grateful to you. But I ain't never owned any such money as that.' 'You mean you ain't got no money?' the judge shouts. 'Not that kind o' money,' says Smithers. 'How much you got?" the judge wants to know.

"Well, Smithers empties his pockets. It counts up to forty-three dollars an' sixty cents. 'The court takes forty dollars on 'count,' the judge barks. 'Three-sixty'll get you to the junction. Lock him up, Sheriff. An' remember, James Smithers, if you're ever seen in this county agin, you'll serve them two years at hard labor.'

"Now, there's a right smart crowd at the stage to see Smithers off next mornin'. 'Course, they're mostly Knights o' the Spur. The gent from Denver don't look much like he did when I first see him. Sheriff tells us afterward as how Smithers had begged for soap an' hot water to scrub his face. Sheriff tells him he's sorry, but the water was all froze up. 'Course, he'd done the best he could with them goose feathers, but his face was still plastered with down. Looked like he'd lathered his face, an' forgot to shave.

"Well, the sheriff's leadin' Smithers up to the stage when Hank Summers steps in. 'Just a minute, Sheriff,' says he. 'Seems like your prisoner might o' forgot somethin' .' 'I ain't forgot nothin',' Smithers snorts, 'an I ain't likely to, neither.' 'Yep,' says Hank, 'you're forgettin' as how them pants you got on belong to me. Reckon you ain't minded to remember a little bet we made in the Silver Star.'

"Smithers looks down at them fancy pants mighty sad-like, an' says, 'Nope, I ain't forgot. But I can't do nothin' 'bout it now. I'll send 'em to you – soon's I get another pair.' 'Nope,' says Hank, 'I'll take 'em now.' Smithers looks at the crowd, sort o' helpless-like. Hopin' somebody might take pity on him, I reckon,

"But somebody yells, 'Better take 'em off, hoss-thief, if you know what's good for you.' Well, Smithers unhitches the pants, an' kicks 'em off. Then the crowd roars, while the sheriff hustles Smithers onto the stage. You see, the gent from the big city was still wearin' his winter flannels. An' they was red as a bull's tongue."

# A Modern Jonah

THE GUESTS ON THE VERANDA were unusually quiet this evening. Some of them were looking upon this land of mystic color for the first time. Therefore, it was hardly to be wondered at if they were somewhat awed by the quiet immensity of their surroundings. The distracted world of man seemed far off indeed in this peaceful valley.

The most recent arrival at the ranch had taken her seat on the steps. Her gaze was intent upon the stars when Jim Dawson took his accustomed place. When her eyes finally came back to earthly objects, she was visibly startled, for she had heard no approaching step.

"Why, ma'am, you look like you might've seen a ghost," Jim remarked, with a reassuring smile.

"I thought I had," she returned, with a nervous glance at her fellow guests. With a sigh, she turned her gaze upon the shadowy bulk of Black Mountain. Then she heard someone saying, "Jim, your friend is late reporting tonight."

"You mean Jonah," Jim responded, with a grin. "Oh, he'll be 'long directly. Reckon mebbe he's havin' trouble gettin' the kids to sleep." The new guest's inquiring gaze was now upon the speaker.

"Oh, here he comes now." She turned to follow Jim's gaze, seeing nothing but the shadows of night. Every passing

moment added an edge to her nerves. Wide eyes returned to the old wrangler, to see him calmly rolling a cigarette. Then – she saw it!

The new guest quit her seat with a shriek. of horror. The action had been rather amazing for one of her generous proportions. "Oh, good heavens," she cried, "drive that awful thing away!"

What she had seen was a toad, also of unusual proportions. It had hopped up the steps, and taken a seat only a few feet from the one she had so hastily left.

"Now, ma'am," Jim was saying, "there ain't no need to be disturbed This feller's just as harmless as a baby. Fact is, he's a heap better-behaved."

With a helpless gesture, the guest sank into the first available chair, while Jim continued: "You see, ma'am, Jonah's one o' the family. An' he comes out every evenin' to listen to the gossip. He likes folks. Reckon our chatter sort o' amuses him. Ain't that right, feller!" and Jim's long fingers stroked the toad's broad back. To all appearances, this wise-looking fellow fully appreciated the human touch.

The guest finally found voice to protest. "Well, I see no sense in keeping a thing like that around to frighten people."

"We're mighty sorry, ma'am," Jim gravely returned. "We shore wasn't aimin' to scare you, was we, Jonah?" and once again he stroked the toad's back.

"He's certainly a fine-looking specimen," another guest remarked. "Was there any special reason for his name?"

"Yep there shore was."

Gipsy had just joined the group, and as she took a chair, she said, "This is one of Jim's stories that I can vouch for. Let us have it, Jim."

"Well, it come 'bout like this," Jim began. Jonah's eyes, glistening in the starlight, were fixed intently on the speaker. "I'm goin' down to the pumphouse one mornin'. On my way I see a young rattler tryin' to drag himself under a bush. He ain't actin' natural, so I take a closer squint. I see he's got quite a swellin' in his middle. An' he's squirmin' like a kid with a belly full o' green apples. Now, if he'd been a bull snake I might o' give him a dose o' paregoric. But him bein' a rattler, I just put him out o' his misery."

"Why, Jim," someone exclaimed, "I thought you were opposed to killing snakes."

"That's right. Generally speakin', that is. When them rattlers stay back in the hills where they belong, we don't bother 'em. But we don't like 'em prowlin' 'round the ranch. You see, some folks don't seem to crave their company.

"Well, as I was sayin', I fix Mister Rattler. Then I get sort o' curious regardin' what's give him such a belly ache. An' when I slit him open, out pops a toad. He blinks a couple o' times, an' looks up at me like he was sayin', 'Thanks, old-timer, that was a close shave.'

" 'Course, he's growed a lot, since then. Reckon that ain't surprisin', though. He ain't got nothin' to do but sit in the flowerbeds all day, stuffin' himself with bugs. An' you can see for yourselves how it was. There just wasn't but one name fittin' for the little feller, an' that was Jonah."

# Trotterville

HE DUDES WERE RESTING IN
the shade of a juniper this afternoon, when someone remarked, "I don't
suppose anyone lives back in these hills."

"Oh, shore," was Jim Dawson's drawling reply. "Trotterville ain't much
more'n a stone's throw from here."

"Trotterville," the dude repeated, with evident surprise. "Why, I thought
Skull Valley was the only settlement around here."

"Nope, not quite," Jim replied, with a suspicious grin. " 'Course this
place ain't as big as Skull Valley. The last census give it two inhabitants.
An' they ain't on speakin' terms, so you can see, it ain't what you'd rightly
call a sociable place."

"What is it, a ghost town?"

"Nope, I wouldn't hardly call it that. There's a mine there. An' it's still
operatin'. That is, when ol' Jake Trotter feels like workin'."

"This sounds interesting," the dude returned. "Tell us why these two
citizens are so unfriendly."

"Now, that's somethin' I don't reckon anybody can tell you. Leastwise,
if they know, they shore ain't talkin'. You see, these fellers – brothers, they
is – come in here a few years back, an' locate in Powder Gulch. Claim they
find a vein o' silver. Anyways, they open a hole in the mountain, build 'em
a shack, an' settle down.

"Folks say it seems like they was gettin' 'long all right, when all o' a
sudden the partnership busts up. The Trotters don't give no reason for the

split, an' folks ain't askin'. They do a lot o' wonderin', though, 'specially when they find out how things was split up. It shore looked like brother Bill had got the worst o' the deal. Jake takes the mine, leavin' Bill with the cabin an' a ol' gas-wagon what can't much more'n limp down to the village onct a month.

"But it don't seem to bother brother Bill none. Reckon mebbe he'd got tired grubbin' for the shiny stuff. Anyways, he seems right well satisfied. Folks claim they ain't spoke to one 'nother since the bust-up.

"Now, it's a right smart tramp to the village, so Jake never goes down no more. Bill does the marketin' for the community. When Jake wants somethin', he scribbles it on a bit o' paper. Then he sticks that paper, 'long with the money, under Bill's door after dark. Then Bill dumps the stuff on Jake's doorstep. It's a right funny system, but it seems to work.

"Jim," someone asked, "could we have a look at this place? You spoke of it being close by."

"Certainly" Gipsy answered, "it isn't far from here." "Yep," Jim agreed, "we can go back that way."

A short while later Jim halted the party, and pointed downward. "There," he said. "That's Trotterville in all her glory."

Silently, the dudes gazed into a narrow gulch. It was rugged enough to appear forbidding, except for the willow trees which fringed the dry wash. A huge walnut tree occupied the center of the stage. And, in grotesque contrast, two crude shacks stood on either side of this monarch.

"Come on, folks," Jim announced, "we'll go down an' call on the boys."

They found only one of the Trotter brothers at home this afternoon. Bill bad gone to the village for supplies. The riders were made welcome, however, by brother Jake.

"Oh, what a relief to get out of that awful wind," one of them remarked, as she took a seat under the big tree. "Mr. Trotter, does the wind ever stop blowing in this country?"

"Yes, ma'am," Jake replied, with a twinkle in his keen eyes. "The wind generally quits blowin' when the rains come."

"And when do the rains come?"

"Well, they generally come along 'bout the time the wind quits blowin'.'"

"I suppose you've done considerable prospecting in your time," came from another of the curious.

"Quite a bit," was the reply. "Spent nigh onto forty years at it. Wasn't always lookin' for gold, though."

"Oh! Diamonds, perhaps?"

"Nope. Never got interested in them stones. Nope, I figure I spent 'bout thirty o' them forty years lookin' for my burros."

"You must have a radio, Mr. Trotter," another dude remarked, observing a wire stretched from the roofs of the two cabins.

"Oh, yes," Jake returned, "me an' Bill both has radios." "Do you have any favorite programs?"

"Nope. Matter o' fact, I don't like the fool thing."

"Then why do you have one, if you don't like it?"

"Well, I reckon you can charge it to my curiosity."

"Your curiosity! I don't understand."

"Well, it's like this," Jake explained. "Brother Bill, he's always been a great feller for the radio. He turns it on one night – an' out comes a groanin' an' a screechin'. 'Now what in thunder is that?' I ask Bill. 'That,' says he, 'is a sympathy orchestra.' 'Humpf! It shore don't sound very sympathetic to me,' says I. 'Well,' says he, 'that's 'cause you ain't got no sense concernin' music.'

"Well, folks," Jake concluded, "I've been listenin' to that stuff for nigh onto twenty years now. An' I ain't got no sympathy out o' it yet."

# Quite Filling

*T*HE DUDES HAD BEEN TALKING about the oddities in names when someone remarked, "Jim, I imagine you've encountered some queer names in your time."

"Shore, I've bumped into a lot o' curios 'long the trail," Jim replied, with a grin. "'Bout the best one was a feller from Arkansas named Queen."

"Queen," someone interposed. "That's quite a royal name, one I never heard before. Tell us about his highness."

"Well," Jim drawled, "fact is, he shore wasn't what you'd be apt to call high. He was full-growed, but sort o' whittled off at both ends, if you get my meanin'. Now this Queen feller generally wore the lead name o' Duke. But that wasn't the name his folks had wished on him. Nope, his right name was Deuce. Deuce Queen, nothin' more nor less."

"What a name!" someone interrupted. "How could a mother do such a thing to her child?"

"She didn't," Jim explained. "She hadn't nothin' to do with it, leastwise, not 'cordin' to Duke. We ask him 'bout it one time, an' this is the story he give us. Seems like his folks had agreed 'bout namin' the kids 'fore any was batched. Dad was to name the boys, an' Ma was to name the gals. Well, the first was a boy. Dad Queen says, seein' as how the cards had always been mighty good to him, an' since he'd hooked up with a gal named King, this young feller's name better be Ace. Then 'long come another boy, an' he gets the name Jack. The third kid turns out to be a boy, too. But this one ain't much bigger'n a well-fed gopher. When his dad first sees him, he blinks a minute, an' says, 'Now that's a deuce o' a lookin' thing, ain't it?' So Deuce was the name they give him.

"I ask the Duke what he thought his dad would've done, if there'd been another boy. 'Don't reckon that would've bothered him,' says Duke. 'You see, he still had the joker.' "

"Were there no girls in the family?" one of the dudes asked.

"Nope, no gals. Duke told us one o' the neighbors had asked his ma what she'd call a gal, if one come 'long. 'Oh,' says she, 'I couldn't think o' breakin' the charm. So I reckon I'd call her Diamond.'"

"I suppose father had a dog named Tray," someone remarked.

"Oh, shore," Jim replied, "the ol' man had a dog, all right. But bein' a gal dog, it was called *Ante*."

# Not Without Humor

THE RANCH GUEST HAD BEEN discussing the peculiarities of the Indian this afternoon. One of them insisted that Indians had no sense of humor. Of course, Jim Dawson had been asked for his opinion.

"Oh, I reckon the Injun likes a joke 'bout as well as anybody," he had told them.

"What makes you think they have a sense of humor?" the dude asked. "I have yet to see one smile."

"Yep," Jim admitted, "Injuns does look sort o' glum-like most o' the time. But that's only 'cause they're thinkin'. Them fellers shore believe in exercise for their thinkers."

"Can you offer anything in support of that belief?"

"Well, I might give you a story I got from ol' Foxear onct." There was an instant demand for the story. Jim shifted his position, and started a fresh cigarette.

"Now," he finally began "I ain't aimin' to give you this story the way it come to me. You see, Injuns is great for mixin' signs with their talkin'. An' thats one thing they ain't found room for in modern schoolin'. Leastwise, I ain't never heard o' it.

"Anyways, Foxy tells it somethin' like this. The chief o' the tribe he belongs to is called Moondog. Now the chief has a daughter, an' her name's Redfeather. She's a right likely-lookin' gal, time she's ripe for marryin', Foxy says. An', with Injuns, that's a right early age.

"Well, this Redfeather she falls in love with a brave called Slofoot. But Moondog, he says nothin' doin' on this marryin' business. Slofoot ain't nowise fit for a chief's daughter, says he. You see, this brave had got hurt when he was little, an' one o' his legs was a might stiff. That sort o' slowed him down, an' kept him out o' the games. That's why he got the name Slofoot. But, 'cordin to Foxear, this Slofoot was a mighty wise feller. Some thought be was most nigh as wise as the chief.

"Foxy says be had a hunch as how there was other reasons for the chief refusin' to give his gal to, Slofoot. This Moondog is mighty fond o' red-eye, an' a heap too chummy with the evil-eyed hombre what runs the tradin' post.

"Now, Slofoot knows Redfeather loves him, an' he's shore up to his eyes in Jove with her. But there ain't nothin' they can do 'bout it. Well, time slides by, as she generally does. An' Foxy's hunch turns out to be right as a mule's off ear. Ol' Moondog makes a deal with the trader. He trades his buddin' daughter for some ammunition, an' a jug o red-eye.

"Foxy says Redfeather was just comin' into bloom when the trader packs her off to the post. But the buds don't open. Nope, she just dries up. An' it ain't no time till she's lookin' like a ol' squaw. Now, the day Redfeather leaves her people, Slofoot up an' leaves, too. Swears he'll never look. at another woman. Likewise he swears he'll get even with the trader someday. n' that brave was never seen with his own people agin. Nobody ever knowed where he took himself. All they knowed, 'cordin' to Foxy, was his droppin' in on the tradin' post each spring, like a bluebird out o' nowheres.

"It looked like Slofoot just come to do a little checkin' up. Had to see how his ladylove was doin', I reckon. How it was tough 'nough on Slofoot in the beginnin', but seein' Redfeather fadin' like she is just 'bout busts his heart. Well, he gets himself some tobacco, or somethin', an' just sits out in front o' the store watchin' for the gal he'd lost. If they happen to meet, they don't say nothin'. Don't reckon they has to. Each one knows what the other' lonely heart is whisperin', more'n likely.

"Well, Foxy says three or four winters has come an' went when Slofoot drops off at the tradin' post one big spring day. It was sort o' like he'd dropped out o' the sky. An' what he sees most nigh burns him up. Redfeather looks mighty nigh as old as his mother when he last seen her. Slofoot figures this can't go on no longer. He's got to do somethin' 'bout it, but he don't know what. Most o' the day he sits on that rickety ol' bench, puffin' his pipe, an' doin' a heap o' thinkin'. An' the more he thinks, the madder he gets.

"Now, Foxy says it's late afternoon when Mister Trader comes out an' takes him a seat on that bench. Slofoot sizes him up out o' the comer o' his eye, an' lets his pipe go out. They sit there quite a spell 'fore Slofoot says, 'Business heap good?' He figures to get the white man to talkin'. Mebbe then he can find a way out o' his troubles. The trader grunts. 'Good 'nough,' says he.

"Seems like that grunt has meanin' for Slofoot. Business good, but somethin' else ain't, says he to himself. Out loud he says, 'Business good, white man happy.' 'Business ain't everythin',' Mister Trader snaps back. 'White man have trouble?' Slofoot asks, sort o' unconcerned-like. 'Plenty,' Mister Trader snorts. 'Who wouldn't, with a woman like I got?'

" 'Redfeather heap good woman,' say Slofoot. He's watchin' the sun sinkin' behind the hills. The trader grunts agin. 'Good for nothin',' says he. 'What for she no good?' says Slofoot. 'Sick,' says the trader. 'Can't do no work. Been sick ever since she come here.' 'You no ant?' asks Slofoot. He lights up his pipe agin, beginnin' to feel a mite better.

" 'I shore don't want her,' the trader most nigh shouts. 'Tried to get rid o' her. Sent her back to the tribe, but she wouldn't stay. I shore made a rotten deal when I hooked onto that squaw.'

"Now it's quite a spell 'fore Slofoot says anythin'. His pipe's gone out agin 'fore he says, 'You no want mebbe somebody take her.' Mister Trader squints at Slofoot sort o' sly-like, an' says to him, 'You want her?' 'Mebbe,' says Slofoot, never takin' his eyes off the sunset. 'Mebbe she no go with Slofoot.' 'She ain't got nothin' to say 'bout it,' the trader shouts. He's gettin' all het up by now. 'Look here, Slofoot,' says he, 'if you want that woman, I'll sell her to you.' 'Sell,' says Slofoot. 'You say she no good. What for me buy no-good woman?'

" 'Well, she's worth *somethin'*,' the trader argues. 'I paid a-plenty, an' I've kept her all these years. I got to have somethin' for her.' 'How much?' Slofoot asks, sort o' like he's askin' the price o' beans. 'What you give?' says the trader. Now Slofoot takes plenty o' time loadin' his pipe agin, 'cordin' to the way Foxy tells it. After a spell, he says, 'One blanket – mebbe two.' 'Make it three, an' she's yours,' the trader snaps.

"Slofoot never bats a eye. Just gets up an' slips 'round a corner o' the buildin'. He's back in a minute, leadin' two ponies. He unrolls a pack, an' spreads three blankets on the ground. The trader looks 'em over, an' says, 'Good 'nough. Now take your woman an' get out o' here.' 'Course, he don't know it, but the trader could just as well had everythin' that Injun owned.

"Slofoot says nary a word. He just heads for the trader's cabin. He calls, an' Redfeather, comes out. He makes a few signs. Redfeather looks sort o' puzzled for a minute, then she disappears. She's back right quick, totin' a bundle under her arm, an' most nigh smilin'. Slofoot gives her a lift onto one o' the ponies. He hops on the other, an' heads west. The trader ain't scarce got his breath 'fore them two has disappeared. Sort o' melt into the sunset, I reckon.'

Jim began to roll a cigarette, when someone said, "That surely isn't the end of the story."

"Reckon it ought to be," was the reply. "It's too long already. But it ain't provin' nothin' concernin' a Injun's sense o' humor." When the cigarette was workin to his satisfaction, he continued. "Well, Foxear says three winters has come an went 'fore Slofoot was seen agin. Then he slips into the tradin' post one day, gets himself some tobacco, an' a mess of gay-colored ribbon.

"Now, Mister Trader's rakin' in the silver when he happens to look out the window. An' he most nigh jumps out o' his hide 'cause o' what he sees. Sittin' on a pony out there is a gay-dressed young squaw, laughin' at the antics o' a couple o' kittens. She sort o' reminds the trader o' Redfeather, 'cept she's plump, an' mighty happy-lookin'. An' she's a heap prettier'n Redfeather ever was. 'Course, the trader knows it ain't nothin' for a Injun to have a couple o' squaws, so he ain't nowise surprised.

"Now, 'course, the trader's got himself another woman long 'fore this. His eyes is gettin' sort o' squinty, but they ain't lost nothin' when it comes to good-lookin' women. So he gets to the door pronto to have him a better look. 'Well, ol' fox,' says he, 'where'd you pick up that one? Gosh, ain't she a good looker!'

" 'Me get her from white man,' Slofoot says. 'Now what fool ever let that squaw get 'way from him?' says the trader. 'He must've been drunk.'

" 'Mebbe – mebbe no,' says Slofoot, most nigh grinnin'. "Me give white man three heap good blankets. Mebbe made white man happy.'

" 'What!' Mister Trader shouts. 'You an't tellin' me that's – no, it can't be her.'

"Slofoot slides through the door, sayin', 'Long, long time she called Redfeather. She still Redfeather.' "

# A Matter of Taste

WHAT'S THAT OVER THERE, Mr. Dawson?" The question had been put to Jim by the newcomer who was riding by his side this morning.

"That's a buzzard, Miss."

"Oh, I thought a buzzard was a huge bird, like an eagle." "No, he ain't so big. Mighty useful, though."

"What's that one doing, I wonder?"

"He's havin' himself some breakfast. A nice mess o' fresh meat."

"What kind of meat could he find away out here? We must be miles from the ranch."

"That's rabbit he's havin' this mornin', if my eyes ain't deceivin' me."

"Oh, horrible!"

"Didn't you never eat rabbit?" Jim mildly inquired. "Why, yes — sometimes."

"It wasn't so horrible, was it?"

"Nooo," was the hesitant reply. "Rabbit is excellent, when properly cooked. But that horrid bird is eating it raw."

"Then you like your meat well-done?" "Yes, I do prefer it that way."

"Well," Jim returned, with a twinkle in his lazy eyes, "it looks to me like you ain't bein' fair with Mister Buzzard. You like your meat well-done. Now me, I ain't carin' much one way or 'nother, just so it's meat. But Mister Buzzard, he likes his rare. So you see, Miss, it's just a matter o' taste."

A long silence followed, finally broken by the dude.

"I believe you said the buzzard was a useful bird," she remarked. "What is it good for?"

"Well," Jim drawled, "I don't know how it is where you come from, but out in these parts things is dyin' all the time. Cows, hosses, rabbits an' the like. Now it could be mighty unpleasant sometimes, if it wasn't for them birds what like their meat raw. Yep, a mighty useful citizen, Mister Buzzard is."

# Not Too Important

CONVERSATION HAD SETTLED upon the subject of horses today. That was to be expected, for the dudes had dismounted to rest after their climb to the top of Wild Horse Mesa.

"Jim," one of them said to their guide, "I suppose you still miss your old horse, Barney."

"Yep, I shore do," Jim returned, gazing wistfully across the valley. "Now, Lady's a mighty good hoss, but it ain't likely she'll ever take ol' Barney's place. You see, me an' Barney had mighty nigh growed up together. We'd been together for more'n twenty years. An' it wasn't all work, neither. Nope, we had lots o' fun together. We hadn't been separated for a day in all that time. I felt worse'n a lost dog when Barney left me."

"Why should you feel so badly over the loss of a horse?" someone asked. "There are plenty of good horses."

"That's right," Jim agreed, gazing at the speaker rather sadly, it seemed. "Yep, there's plenty o' good folks too, but a feller ain't apt to be in love with too many o' 'em."

"You don't mean to say you were actually in love with this animal?"

"That's just what I'm sayin', ma'am," was Jim's prompt response. "You see, I never thought o' Barney as bein' a animal. He was my best friend. Me an' Barney'd traveled all over the country together, an' we'd lived together. He never complained if the goin' was tough, or rations was short. He was always faithful an' loyal. Most folks don't understand the loyalty a hoss like that has for his two-legged friend. I wasn't his master, we was pals.

The hardest job I ever had to do was to covet Barney up so I couldn't ever see him no more. But I quit grievin' for him – after I come to my senses."

"How was that?" someone asked. "How did you become reconciled to your loss?"

"Well, when I'd thought it over, I was sort o' grateful. I figured it was a lot better havin' Barney go first. You see, a boss ain't got no choice concemin' who he's goin' to live with, an' where. An' I'd shore been unhappy. if Barney'd fallen in with some hombre what wasn't good to him. Yep, the ol' boy had gone home, an' I knowed he was happy, so I had no business complainin'."

"Oh, come now," the dude protested, "you surely don't believe there is a hereafter for animals."

"Yep, I shore do. Leastwise, for bosses an' dogs. Why shouldn't there be? They got a right to their reward in a better place than this ol' world. An' folks shore ain't got no corner on the virtues. A good hoss shore has a lot more in his favor than a heap o' folks I've knowed."

"Well, I for one certainly wouldn't argue that point," one of Jim's friends remarked. "But to get back to Barney again. I once heard you tell the story of the time you were cornered by wolves. You said this Barney horse was not afraid of fire. Now, Jim, that was something I could not accept. I was brought up to believe that horses had an instinctive fear of fire, and they never got over it."

"I believed that too," Jim replied, "till I got 'quainted with Barney. If he ever had any fear, he shore got over it. He could enjoy a campfire on a cold night 'bout as well as anybody. An' he was smart 'nough to know the difference 'tween a good fire an' a bad one. Like the time we was crossin' southern Utah." The dudes waited expectantly, while Jim rolled a cigarette.

"We'd stopped at a ranch 'bout noontime," he finally began. "Barney, he lunches on a mess o' barley, an' I stretch my belt considerable with good Mormon cookin'. Well, we hit a stretch o' mighty barren country after leavin' the ranch. When night catches up with us I ain't too shore where we are, so we just quit for the day. It was warm, an' I wasn't too hungry, so I don't bother buildin' a fire. Just make my meal on a slice o' jerky an' some cold biscuits the rancher's wife had give me.

"I make me a cigarette, stretch out on the ground an' pull a blanket over me. The stars is makin' plenty o' light, an' I can see Barney ain't far off. He's munchin' at a patch o' grama grass. I'm still thinkin' 'bout that fried ham I'd bad at noon when my eyes quit blinkin'. An' I'm havin' me a right pleasant dream when I'm waked by a snortin', an' a scrapin' noise close by.

"Well, I reckon I could give you forty chances an' you wouldn't be apt to guess what I see when I get my eyes open. You see, that cigarette had slipped out o' my fingers, an' set fire to the dry grass. An' there was that Barney hoss doin' his best to stomp it out. He knowed mighty well that was no campfire, an it hadn't no business there."

"That makes a good story, Dawson," one of the dudes remarked, "but you surely don't expect anyone to believe it."

"Well," Jim drawled, as he got to his feet, "I'll just give you the answer I heard my granddad give to that same question onct. 'Well,' says he, 'I don't reckon it makes much difference if you believe it or not. It shore ain't goin' to make no change in the comin' election.' "

# *The Parson*

*I*T WAS NEARING THE FIRST
of September, and the nights were becoming chilly. The guests were
gathered about a fire which Jim Dawson had built near the patio this
evening. Someone opened the conversation by remarking:

"Jim, I suppose you knew many of the big gamblers, in the old days."

"Yep," Jim replied, taking his usual seat, "I used to meet up with some
o' the big boys now an' agin."

"They must have been very picturesque characters. Could you tell us
something about them?"

"Well, I might give you a squint at The Parson," Jim returned, rolling
a cigarette with one hand, while he scratched an ear with the other. "I
knowed The Parson right well."

"That's quite a name for a gambler. Was he a friend of yours?" The
creases about Jim's eyes deepened, as he gazed thoughtfully into the fire.

"Oh, no," he said, "we wasn't what you could rightly call friends. I just
happen to meet up with The Parson more'n any o' the rest o' the big
fellers. I done a heap o' roamin' them days, an' it seemed like The Parson
was right fond o' travelin' too. He never stayed long in one place. Nobody
knowed just why that was, for shore, but 'course, they had their 'spicions.

"Well, this feller's name was Daniel Parsons. Leastwise, that's what he
claims it is. The story was that he started out to be a preacher. But the
pickin' was too lean for the way he had in mind to be livin'. So he throws
in with the bankin' business. 'Course, that story could been hatched up

just 'cause o' the name what was hung onto him. Anyways, he was best knowed as The Parson, an' he didn't seem to have no objections to goin' by that name.

"This Parson was shore quite a feller. You wouldn't never took him for a gambler. Most o' the big fellers I met up with looked like they hadn't never been used to eatin' much 'cept carpet tacks an' vinegar. But that shore didn't hold with The Parson. I never seen him when he wasn't smilin'. An' he could keep a crowd laughin' till their shirts was soaked with tears. Reckon mebbe that was some help to him in his dealin'.

"But, be that as she could, as Granddad used to say, The Parson was shore one slick hombre. Yep, just 'bout as slick as grease on a hot skillet. If a feller had jacks or queens up, The Parson was in with kings. An' if it was kings up, he could generally arrange to have aces. 'Course, he'd lose a hand now an' agin. But that never bothered The Parson. He just laughed all the louder.

"Now the last time I see The Parson he's operatin' up in Montana. Quite a spell after that I meet up with a ol' friend o' mine from Texas. He knowed The Parson 'bout as well as anybody, I reckon, an' this is the story he give me.

"Quite a few winters has passed over The Parson's head. An' his 'quaintance has growed to where it's becomin' sort o' uncomfortable you might say. So he figures he might be doin' right well if he was to change his callin', an' settle down somewheres. 'Next thing we know –,' says my friend, 'The Parson's operatin' a cemetery in Colorado.'

"Well, it seems like The Parson hears 'bout a gold strike while he's up in Montana. So he figures to go down an' have him a look. The Parson was always a slow movin' feller, an' he still is. He don't come down by stage. He's straddlin' a hoss when he sets out, an' he's stickin' to the least traveled trails. He's takin' his time, 'cause there's a lot o' interestin' places 'long the way what he ain't never seen. So, by the time he gets to Rock Point – that's the name o' this place in Colorado – several moons has come an' went. He finds the townsite's 'bout all took up, an' business is shore flourishin'.

"The Parson looks over the hills a bit, but don't find nothin' what's got much tradin' value. Fact is, though, he ain't interested in gold. What he's after is a idee. He's cravin' a proposition with plenty o' income an' no work. You see, The Parson hadn't been brung up on work, an' somehow or other he'd never got 'quainted with it. Now he's been 'round 'nough minin' camps to know folks ain't generally got no time to be gettin' sick. So the doctor business is out. 'Course, killin' gets to most nigh epidemic proportions in them places, but he figures undertakin' ain't too appetizin', So he scratches that one off the list. He's 'bout to give up, and go back to bis ol' callin', when he stumbles onto a bit o' land.

"Now, when I say land, I'm meanin' somethin' with dirt on it, 'stead o' rock. A little snoopin' shows The Parson he's found the only thing o' the kind for miles an' miles. Folks has been so busy scrambling for gold they ain't give no thought to a restin' place for the dead. So The Parson tacks onto this place pronto. He stakes him a claim, builds him a fence 'round it, an' hangs up a shingle. That there shingle reads like this: *THE PARSON'S CEMETERY – Buryin' lots 8 x 10 feet, $1000 per.*

"Well, it's early spring when The Parson lands in Rock Point. An' by late fall that year he's got so much money it most nigh makes him dizzy thinkin' 'bout it. He ain't trustin' his local brethren, neither. Nope, he's got that money cached in Denver. So he figures mebbe it wouldn't be a bad notion if he was to slip into Denver to see if the place still looks safe. He sort o' feels in need o' a change o' air, anyways.

"Now, The Parson's goin' down the main street in Denver one mornin' to have him a peek at the bank where he's got his money. 'Fore he gets there it starts rainin'. The Parson always wore good clothes, an' not hankerin' to have 'em spoiled, he steps into the post office. He stands there lookin' out the window, hopin' the rain don't last long. But it looks sort o' like that rain had moved in for the day, so he looks 'round for a place to sit.

He don't see nothin' invitin', but he sees somethin' else. An' them sharp eyes o' his starts blinkin' overtime."

Jim shifted his position, and began to roll a cigarette. The dudes waited, but not too patiently. "Well," he continued, "The Parson's rovin' eyes had lit on the picture gallery. An' there was one picture in that collection what makes him feel sort o' creepy when he looks close. It had most likely been hangin' there for quite a spell, 'cause the gent's name was 'bout wore off. But The Parson wasn't concernin' himself 'bout names. He was mighty good at rememberin' faces, an' he shore hadn't no call to be forgettin' the one he was lookin' at. It had been lookin' back at him from a mirror for too many years. This was a gent what had onct got too chummy with a stage totin' U.S. mail, an' the law seemed to have a great yearnin' for him.

"Now it seems The Parson forgets the rain all o' a sudden. Anyways, he don't lose no time relocatin' himself." At this point Jim had to relight his cigarette. "Queer, ain't it," he finally concluded, "how a feller's memory can stampede sometimes? Well, I reckon that's how it was with The Parson. Anyways, he forgets to go back to Rock Point. He takes the first stage headin' south. An' the last we hear o' The Parson, he's took up his residence in Mexico."

# Riders in the Sky

$\mathcal{A}$ FEW FLEECY CLOUDS DRIFT-
ed out of the southwest this evening. They were tinted with an indescrib-
able blend of crimson and gold, as the sun had dipped out of sight behind
Black Mountain. And perhaps that was what had prompted Jim Dawson
to sing *Ghost Riders in the Sky*.

When the song was finished, someone remarked, "Isn't that fantastic?"

"Well, I wouldn't know, ma'am," Jim drawled. "Don't seem to recall
ever meetin' up with anybody by that name. Used to know a Fan Tanner
down in Texas. Don't reckon they was related, though."

"Jim," one of his friends asked, "why hasn't that song been more
popular?"

"Mebbe it's 'cause it ain't too easy to sing," Jim offered. "Looks to me
like a feller ain't got no business tryin' it, 'less he sort o' feels what he's
singin' 'bout."

"I can't agree," came from the first dude. "As I said, it's fantastic. It's
much too unreal for general acceptance."

"Now, mebbe you ain't understandin' it," Jim returned. "You see, that
song is picturin' a dream. An' dreams shore ain't real. Generally speakin',
that is. Mebbe I ain't the feller to be sayin' it. But 'cordin' to my way o'
thinkin', that's one o' the best songs ever written 'bout this country. You
ain't likely to be hearin' many folks singin' it, but that ain't goin' to keep
it from livin' long after we're gone."

"I hardly believe you'll find much agreement with your opinion," the dude persisted. "But why do you say I don't understand it?"

"Well, ma'am," Jim thoughtfully replied, "I reckon it's 'cause you just ain't 'quainted with what went into that song. You sort o' got to see the picture to understand the full meanin'. 'Course, that's easy for me. Now, I can see myself out on the plains; or in some canyon, mebbe. Been chasin' steers all day; no time to think o' nothin' else. Sweatin', an' doin' a heap o' cussin' mebbe. I'm stretched out for the night now. My saddle's the softest pillow I can find, an' I ain't wearin' no pajamas. My shirt ain't dried out yet, an' I can still smell them steers.

"There ain't no coverin' over me, 'cept the heavens. A few clouds is driftin' by, an' they're still holdin' some o' the color left over from the settin' sun. I can see all sorts o' shapes in them clouds. Yep, I see steers' horns, an' hoss tails, an' a heap o' queer-lookin' things comin' an' gain'.

"Well, I'm gettin' mighty sleepy, an' my eyes go shut. But 'fore I'm lost I get to thinkin'. Thinkin' 'bout some o' the big times I've had. Thinkin' 'bout some what wasn't so nice, mebbe, an' I wouldn't mind forgettin' 'em.

"Now, folks, I've heard as how there ain't nothin' in this life what don't add up to somethin'. An' it shore looks to me like we got the makin's now. There's two pictures in my mind when I go slumberin'. It ain't no trick for 'em to get together in dreamland. An' there you have it – *Ghost Riders in the Sky.*"

Riders in the Sky

# A Wild Ride

JIM DAWSON PUT DOWN THE guitar while he rolled a cigarette. The stars were so brilliant. and appeared so close, that silence had followed the last song. Jim had sung one of his old favorites, *The Stars Are Watching.*

The silence was finally broken by one of his friends. "Jim," he said, "I've listened to a great many of your stories, but I never heard you mention anything concerning a stampede. I'm wondering if you might be holding out on us."

Jim lit a cigarette before replying. "Nope, I ain't been holdin' out on you, leastwise not meanin' to. I reckon it's 'cause o' me not bein' mixed up with many o' them unhappy shows."

"Couldn't you tell us something about them?" his friend asked. Jim gazed thoughtfully up at the stars.

"Well," he finally replied, "when a big bunch o' cattle takes a notion to stampede, it's generally somethin'. a feller sort o' likes to forget. But I was caught in one what I shore ain't apt to be forgettin'. I can't figure how you're likely to be interested in me tellin' 'bout it. But since you've asked for it, here it is.

"Now, this was 'way back when I was workin' for the Flyin' X outfit up in Montana. We're drivin' 'bout a thousand head o' steers to the railroad. Been out three or four days, an' everythin's went fine. I'm night-herdin', 'long with a feller called Possum Jones. Now Possum, he takes over the watch 'bout midnight, an' I move into camp to catch me some coffee an' a bit o' sleep.

"A feller couldn't ask for a better contented lot o' cattle than that herd was. There was plenty o' feed an' water 'long the trail, an' we shore hadn't no reason to be lookin' for trouble. Well, everythin's so peaceful-like, Possum ain't got nothin' to keep him busy. He says he gets so sleepy he just can't keep bis blinkers open. So he figures he might as well catch him a siesta. So he just eases to one side o' his saddle. an' dozes off. Possum says he must've slid too much weight onto that stirrup while he's dozin'. Anyways, the stirrup leather snaps. An' that's all it takes to set off the fireworks with a herd o' longhorns.

"Well, them critters is on their feet most nigh as quick as a feller can draw a six-shooter. An' they're off like a flock o' blackbirds. They ain't got no notion, where they're gain', but its a cinch thay ain't aimin' to pull up 'fore dayliaht.

"Now, by the time I get it into my sleepy head that the roarin' what's hit my ears ain't no dream, it' too late. Them bellerin' longhorns is most nigh on top o' me, headin' straight for the camp.

"Well, I just got sense 'nough to know there ain't no use tryin' to outrun them critters. But the chuck wagon ain't too far off, an' it shore looks mighty good to me right now. In less time than I'm takin' in the tellin', I'm sprawled out on top o' that ol' friend. Now, it shore wasn't no thinkin' of mine what put me up there. Right then it seemed like I didn't own a thinker. Nope, I was just hopin'. Hopin' the wagon might split that roarin' herd.

"Well, it did, but not for long. Reckon mebbe half the herd had pounded by when one o' them two-yard born caught a wheel – an' over we go. Pots an' pans is rattlin', canvas rippin', an' wood crackin' like pistol hot. Mixed with the bellerin' o' them steers, it makes quite a chorus. But it shore ain't no melody.

"Now, I'm wonderin' what kind o' report I'm goin' to make to ol' Saint Pete when I pull up at the pearly gates. But I make a landin' quicker'n I'm expectin'. 'Course, I figure I've hit' the ground, an' my thinkin' time ain't apt to be long drawed out. But I keep on breathin'. An' all o' a sudden it comes to me as how the ground ain't in the habit o' movin'. Generally speakin', that is. An' I'm shore movin'."

The dudes were forced to wait impatiently while Jim took time out to roll a cigarette. "Well," he finally resumed. "it's a lucky thing for me my wits ain't scattered too far by that rough landin'. I know there ain't but one place I can be, an' that's on the back o' one o' them longhorns.

"That critter ain't no rockin' chair, I'm tellin' you, but I shore ain't complainin'. Nope, I'm plenty grateful. You see, I've got two horns to hang onto now, 'stead o' just one. Now, it ain't a dark night, 'cause there ain't a cloud in the sky the last time I seen it. But them racin' steers is kickin' up so much dust I can't even see the horns in front o' me. Fact is, though, I ain't tryin' to see nothin'. I'm keepin' my peepers tight shut. An' I'm hopin' my lungs ain't goin' to be plugged up by that ill-smellin' dust. Likewise, I'm hopin' one o' them longhorns don't take a notion to scrape me off my roostin' place.

"Well, we been goin' for quite a long spell when somethin' tickles my misty thinker. There's a big critter on my off side what keeps crowdin' me so close I get to wonderin' 'bout it. I can't see him, 'course, but I know he's big 'cause o' the way his ribs is scrapin' my knee. An' he shore ain't movin' like a steer, neither.

"Now, I ain't got this thing figured out, when I take a squint out o' my dusty peepers. An' what I see is sweeter'n music to my ears — an' that's mighty sweet. I can see day is breakin'. An' I can see the horns I'm grippin'. Then somethin' else gets in my eye. First off, I figure I must be dreamin'. But the longhorns is slowin' down now, an' the dust ain't quite so thick. It's gettin' lighter, too.

"Nope, I ain't been dreamin'. My big travelin' companion ain't no steer. An' I don't reckon I was ever so glad to see anythin' in all my life. All o' a sudden my eyes get a good washin'. Reckon that can happen to 'most anybody now an' agin. 'Specially when he meets up with a ol' friend he ain't countin' on ever seein' agin. Well, with me it's just 'cause I'm lookin' at the best boss I ever straddled. How Barney got there is more'n I can tell you – but there he was. An' he shore looks pleased with himself when I speak to him. He ain't got no saddle, an' no bridle, but I shore ain't upset 'bout that. After ridin' that longhorn a good part o' the night, Barney's goin' to feel like a featherbed.

"Well, folks," Jim concluded, "that's 'bout it. Them longhorns put on the brakes at a water hole. Now that water ain't none too appetizin', but me an' Barney have a drink together. By that time it's light 'nough for me to have a good look. An' mebbe you ain't minded to believe it, but them pesky critters had pulled up at the loadin' station we'd been headin' for."

# A Soft Answer

*D*ARKNESS WAS FAST SETTL-
ing upon the ranch when Jim Dawson left the bunkhouse this evening. He
was later than usual in joining the guests on the veranda. That fact had
not prompted any haste on his part, however. In fact, his movements were
never hurried. He was much like an Indian, in many respects, especially
his walk. His slow, graceful stride was almost noiseless.

With the timeworn guitar under his arm, he was nearing one of the
guest cabins when the door opened, and two indistinct forms stepped into
the gathering night. They were mere shadows in the gloom, but their
identity was revealed to Jim by their incautious voices. These two had
arrived only a few days before, mother and daughter on their first visit
to Rainbow.

The mother had let it be known that this long trip from the far East
was not of her choosing. And it was quite evident that she was decidedly
uncomfortable so far from her natural habitat. Her horse-loving daughter
had been responsible for this venture into a strange and uncouth land.

"I suppose," she was now saying, "we will have to listen to that boresome
cowboy again; with his crude stories, and that atrocious guitar."

'Why, Mother," the daughter protested, "I find Mr. Dawson rather
amusing. And I have heard much worse music."

"Amusing! Humpf!" was the prompt retort. "That man is nothing but
a conceited monkey, in my opinion."

Jim Dawson might have heard considerably more concerning himself had he not intentionally kicked a stone in his path. Smothered exclamations followed, as the women whirled to face the oncoming shadow. Their faces were mercifully hidden in the gloom.

"Evenin', folks," came to their startled ears in a soft drawl.

"Oh, good evening, Mr. Dawson," the daughter returned, when she had recovered from her surprise.

"A right charitable evenin', this," Jim declared, as he closed the short distance between them.

"Charitable?" was the somewhat hesitant return. "I don't believe I understand you."

"Well," came the oft-spoken reply, "an evenin' like this makes a person feel so good he's most nigh tempted to be lovin' his worst enemy."

# A Clean Nose

THAT BRIEF AND SHADOWY encounter with Jim Dawson had given Mrs. Blank something to think about. She was almost tempted to believe that Rainbow's wrangler might not be as crude as he appeared. She was unwilling to admit anything openly, however. No, nothing, except that he had aroused her curiosity.

A few days later, Jim was at the barn making preparations for a moonlight picnic. He was more than surprised when Miss Blank appeared to inquire if it would be possible for her mother to go along in the chuck wagon.

"Why, shore," Jim said. "But she's takin' on somethin' she ain't apt to forget in a hurry. It's a rough trip. An' this ol' wagon shore ain't no Pullman car."

"Yes, I know," was the laughing reply. "I rode one once. But Mother seems quite determined.

With pillows and blankets, Jim did what he could to put a little comfort to the board seat of the wagon. He smiled at this unexpected turn of events.

The chuck wagon had preceded the riders. When the latter had reached the end of their climb to the mesa, they received a cheery greeting from Mrs. Blank. In apparent contentment, and none the worse for her trip, she was seated on a pile of blankets watching the building of the campfire. Turning their horses loose, the dudes quickly made themselves comfortable. Many of them might have found it difficult to say which was the more interesting, the leisurely unfolding of the sunset, or Jim Dawson's skillful preparation of the coming meal.

"Well, folks," he finally announced, "there it is. Fill up your platters." Jim was already heaping a plate with steaming beans, crisp bacon and biscuits.

Mrs. Blank nudged her daughter. "Will you look at that," she whispered. "Oooh, these crude Westerners!" Miss Blank rose, as Jim, with plate in hand, approached them. Mrs. Blank shrugged her shoulders in resignation. With a gracious ease and a warm smile, Jim proffered the generous plate. Mrs. Blank's self-possession deserted her for an instant. "Oh, thank you," she finally managed. Her eyes dropped to the plate to hide her confusion, as she added, "You are very thoughtful, Mr. Dawson."

"Well, I don't reckon it hurts a feller to be exercisin' his thinker now an' agin. That is, if he's got one." And with that smiling response, Jim filled a plate for himself, and took a seat beside one of his old friends.

As lusty appetites were appeased, conversation grew more lively. It finally settled upon world affairs, revealing a sharp difference of opinion regarding the moral trend.

"Jim," his friend asked, "what's your opinion? Do you think the world is getting better, or worse?"

"Well," came the thoughtful reply, "I don't reckon I ought to be sayin'. I don't see much o' the world, you know."

"Yes, but you read. And you come in contact with people from all over. You must have an opinion on the question."

"Well, so far as I can see, it looks sort o' like this. Mebbe the ol' world's gettin' better. But if it is, it shore ain't no epidemic."

"I think we can all agree on that," came from another dude. "But tell us, if you will, what you would suggest to improve this unfortunate situation."

"Pardon me," Jim returned, "but I ain't givin' out no suggestions. It looks to me as how Jim Dawson might be doin' a right good job just mindin' his own business."

"Why, Dawson," someone exclaimed, "you're a philosopher!"

"No, ma'am," was the prompt response. "I'm a Republican." The conversation was becoming too serious to suit Jim.

"A Republican! Why, I thought you were a Texan."

"Yep, I'm all o' that, too. By rights, I reckon. Folks was all Democrats, too. Might've been one myself, I reckon, if I hadn't left home when I did. You see, I pulled stakes 'fore I was ol' 'nough to be branded. An' mebbe I'd been a Democrat anyways, if I hadn't met up with Teddy Roosevelt."

"Oh, how interesting!" came unexpectedly from Mrs. Blank. "Please tell us about your meeting with that fascinating character."

"Well, there ain't so much to tell," Jim drawled, rolling a fresh cigarette. "I run into Teddy one mornin', an' like a lot o' hoss-straddlers, 'fore night-fall I was wearin' the R. R. brand."

"The Rough Riders!" Jim's friend exclaimed. "Why, I didn't know you had seen service, Jim."

"Nope, never did," was the sorrowful response. "Leastwise, not the kind you're thinkin' on. All the service I ever seen was in a Florida hospital. You see, I busted a leg just 'fore the outfit was leavin' for Cuba. When I get so I can hobble 'round agin, they make me a orderly, or somethin'. Keep me there nursemaidin' till the war's over. But I ain't kickin'. That is, I ain't now, 'cause I learned somethin'. Reckon a feller ought to learn somethin' now an' agin, if he's got the sense o' a gopher."

"Would you mind telling us what you learned from that experience?" his friend asked.

"Oh, I reckon there ain't no harm in tellin' it now. Well, the day the boys was pullin' out for Cuba, Teddy comes to the hospital. He comes in to where I'm stretched out, cussin' my luck. An' he says to me, 'Dawson, my boy, I hardly know how we're a goin' to lick them Spaniards without your help, but we'll do the best we can.'

"Well, somehow the Spaniards was licked, all right. An' that was a good lesson for me, I reckon. You see, 'long 'bout that time I was gettin' a mite too big for my pants. An' the war bein' won without no help from me – well, it sort o' took me in a couple o' notches.

"An' so it be with the poor ol' world today. It looks like it was in one awful mess. But somehow, I reckon, it'll have to get 'long as good as it can without much help from me. 'Bout all Jim Dawson can do, I reckon, is try to keep his own nose clean."

# A Sad End

*T*HE BLANKS HAD COME TO THE ranch to stay two weeks, but a month had slipped by before they took their departure. The day before they were to leave, Miss Blank presented Jim Dawson with a slip of blue paper. Jim squinted at it curiously for a minute. It was a check, the amount of which was almost equal to his monthly wage. He smiled, as he heard, "Mother asked me to give that to you."

"Pardon me for askin' what for?" Jim's eyes were still upon the check in his hand.

"She just wanted you to know that she appreciated your part in making our stay here a very enjoyable one."

"That's nice," Jim returned. "I'm glad if you folks has had a good time. But, this ain't called for," and he held out the check. Miss Blank looked puzzled, as she accepted it.

"But what shall I tell Mother?" she asked.

"Just tell her she's already paid in full for everythin'," Jim replied, as he began to roll a cigarette. "You see, Miss Blank, the Lady Boss pays good wages, an' if the help ain't satisfied, they know there ain't nothin' keepin' 'em here. An' I reckon if it was found out we was takin' tips, we'd be gettin' a special invitation to get movin', pronto."

"That's rather old-fashioned, isn't it?"

"Yep, I reckon it is. But it ain't such a bad notion, 'cordin' to my way o' thinkin'. I ain't never fell in with this business o' tippin'. Looks to me sort o' like a holdup, an' I shore ain't aimin' to have no part in it. So if you'll just tell your mother I'm 'preciatin' her intentions, we'll call it square."

One might have thought that would be the end of the matter, but it was not. "Well," Mrs. Blank remarked, as she tore up the check, "that man is certainly rare in my experience. I'm glad we stayed long enough for me to change my opinion of him."

It was some two weeks later that Jim received a small parcel by registered mail. He was considerably annoyed to find that it contained a wrist watch, sent to him by Mrs. Blank. He showed it to Gipsy that evening.

"What am I goin' to do 'bout this?" he asked.

"There is only one thing you can do," Gipsy told him. "Keep it, and write her a letter of thanks."

"Shore," Jim said, with troubled eyes on the gift, "I reckon that's a fine piece o' clockwork. But I've got no more use for it than a louse has for religion. Wish folks wouldn't be sendin' me things."

"But you can't hurt the lady's feelings by sending it back. She wants you to have it, or she would not have sent it."

A few days later Gipsy came to the corral where Jim was preparing for the morning ride. "Jim, where's that watch Mrs. Blank sent you?" she asked. "One of the guests broke his this morning, and seems much disturbed about it. Says he doesn't feel dressed without a watch. Would you mind lending yours?"

"Nope. Be mighty glad to, if I had it."

"What did you do with it?"

"Traded it off last time I was in town."

"What did you trade it for?"

"A saddle blanket."

"One saddle blanket!" Gipsy exclaimed. "Why, man, that watch was worth half a dozen saddle blankets."

"Mebbe so," Jim drawled, "but it shore wasn't worth nothin' to me."

To the surprise of everyone at Rainbow, the Blanks returned the following summer. Mrs. Blank asked Jim one day why he was not wearing the watch she had given him. "Well, ma'am," he explained, "that's too fine a watch to be wearin' every day. A feller sort o' likes to keep such fancy things for special shows. You know, weddin's, funerals, an' the like. An' there's another reason why I ain't wearin' it all the time. You see, I sort o' live with the bosses, you might say. An' bosses has queer notions 'bout some things – 'specially the things folks wear. Now I been wearin' 'bout the same kind o' togs as long as these bosses has knowed me. An' if they was to see me in some fancy outfit, they shore wouldn't be likin' it. An' I'd have my troubles with 'em. So you can see for yourself how it might be. If I was to bust in the corral some mornin' with that watch hangin' on my arm, I could shore figure on a stampede. An' that might be the end o' Jim Dawson."

# Rather Unexpected

*O*NE SUMMER RAINBOW ENTER-
tained two guests who were decidedly literary-minded. In fact, one of
them was a poet of some repute.

This evening, after Jim Dawson had given them some of his favorite
songs, the conversation drifted into poetry. Several original verses had
been offered, when one of the guests said, "Dawson, this must be most
uninteresting to you."

"Oh, no," Jim returned, with a smothered yawn, "it don't bother me."

"I don't suppose you ever read poetry," the guest remarked.

"Oh, shore," was the unexpected reply, "I read some now an' agin. You
see, my dad was a great feller for that stuff. Used to make us kids learn a
poem now an' agin. Claimed it was good brain exercise. Reckon mebbe it
is, if a feller has any brains to work on."

"How interesting!" someone exclaimed. "Do you remember any of those
poems?"

"Well, I reckon I ought. Let's see now," and Jim scratched an ear. "Yep,
I reckon I can still remember the one Dad called, 'Where Do They Go
from Here?' "

"That's one I never heard of. Do you know who wrote it?" the poet asked.

"Nope. It always sounded to me like it might've been one o' Dad's own
makin'. He was right good at that sometimes."

"Well, please let us have it."

"Okay," Jim returned, again thoughtfully scratching an ear. "Now I ain't thought on it in quite a spell, but it seems like it went somethin' like this:

"What comes o' the cowpoke, his chips all in?

Now I'm tellin' you, it ain't no Joke;

This findin' a fittin' restin' place

For the battered an' wore-out cowpoke.

Ain't no use him goin' to Heaven.

He'd have no chance with ol' Saint Pete; Covered with dust, smellin' like a boss,

An' no socks on his unwashed feet.

Now a cowpoke, he's used to boilin' heat.

No use sendin' him where it's a mite hotter. An' if the Devil don't know how tough he is,

Well, believe me, he shore oughter.

Mebbe he comes back in the shape o' a hoss.

Say now, that shore wouldn't be bad. He'd be happy sleepin' on the range,

Thinkin' o' the good times he'd had.

Well, there ain't no way o' knowin'

What comes o' the poor ol' cowpokes. There's just one thing we're shore 'bout;

They ain't a lot like most folks."

# Calling It Quits

*T*HE WAR WAS OVER. IT HAD been over for some time, in fact. That was evidenced by the increase in travel; people were moving about now with something of their onetime freedom.

It was one of those lazy days of late summer. Jim Dawson was on his way to town, because of a letter received the day before. He was going in to meet a good friend, a loyal guest of Rainbow Ranch.

This young person from the nation's capital had been vacationing at a ranch in the southern part of the state. She had written to say that she would be going through Prescott on her way home. And, if convenient to her friends, she would stop off here for a day. Of course, it would be convenient. Decidedly so, for she had been one of the favorite guests at Rainbow for more than one summer.

She had no more than comfortably seated herself beside the old wrangler when she said, "Jim, I'm surprised at you."

"Surprised? Now how could I surprise anybody?"

"Why, getting married the way you did, and never letting your friends know about it until long afterward."

"Well, the fact is," Jim laughingly returned, "our friends knew most nigh as much 'bout it as we did. You see, it was over an' done with most nigh 'fore we knew it ourselves."

"Now, that's almost as clear as the Colorado River."

"Yep, I reckoned it would be. But this is how it come 'bout. The dudes had cleared out 'bout the middle o' November that year. That is, all but a mighty nice couple from Chicago. They stayed on till Thanksgivin'.

"I take 'em to town that day to get the evenin' train. When I get home I find the Lady Boss sittin' in front o' the fire. She speaks to me when I come in, but she don't look up. Mike is layin' close beside her, an' the way that dog looks at me shore tells me there's somethin' out o' gear.

" 'What's the trouble?' I ask, toastin' myself 'fore the fire. 'You look sort o' glum.'

"Then she looks up at me, an' says, 'Jim, I've been sittin' here thinkin' ever since the folks left. An' my thoughts haven't been happy ones. I've come to the conclusion that we might as well call it quits.'

" 'Quits,' says I, tryin' hard to keep my balance. 'What you mean, quits?'

" 'Well,' she says, 'you know how it's been all this year. Oh, yes, a good year, in a way. The busiest year we ever had. Yet –'

"Shore. I knew. She didn't need to tell me. Yep, it had been a mighty busy year. A feller wondered sometimes how the folks managed to get so far from home, travel bein' what it was. All the dude outfits in this part o' the country had give it up, but we hadn't seen a breathin' spell all year.

"A full year. Yep, an' a mighty tough one for the Lady Boss. You know, she was mighty proud o' the table she set, an' had a right to be. But it had been slippin', an' it worried her. Just couldn't get the kind o' feed she was used to servin'. On top o' that, cooks was 'bout as scarce as snakes' ears. An' them what was floatin' 'round wasn't worth their salt.

"Well, that means the Lady Boss has to spend a lot o' time in the kitchen, neglectin' the guests, an' gettin' mighty little ridin'. An' you know what that meant to her. They had 'most everythin' rationed, 'cept the air. Reckon they couldn't figure out no way to handle that article. Oh, shore, it was a fine mess, an' gettin' worse, 'stead o' better.

"When she's through tellin' me all this, she just sits there starin' into the fire. Mike, he sits up an' licks her hand. That's his way o' showin' how he feels 'bout it. Me, I take me a seat, an' do some starin' on my own 'count.

What could a feller say? Seemed like my tongue had slid down my throat, an' my ol' thinker had took off to the next county.

'I'm tellin' you, it shore seemed like hours 'fore I locate that tongue o' mine. When I do, I say to her, 'Now, since you've corralled all the facts in the case, what you aim to do with 'em? What's the next move?'

" 'The only thing I know,' she says, 'is to sell out, an' forget the dude business. Anyways, till the war's over.'

" 'Good 'nough, so far as it goes,' says I. 'But how 'bout you? Where might you be goin', an' what you think you'll be doin' with yourself?'

" 'I don't know,' she says. 'I hadn't thought 'bout that. I'm more concerned 'bout you. What'll you do?'

" 'Me?' says I, doin' my best to squeeze out a laugh. 'Now, don't be botherin' your pretty head 'bout me. I'll find me a hole somewrheres. Always have.'

"Well, she don't say a word, just goes to starin' agin. After a while I says to her, 'Listen, Chiquito. Seein' as neither o' us is headin' for any place in particular, what's to hinder us from goin' together?' "

Silence stepped in. The girl beside Jim Dawson knew him quite well. She waited patiently, gazing intently at the bronzed profile. Then the car rumbled over a cattle guard. It brought her to the sudden realization that they had entered the forest. Stately pine trees were now shading the highway, and she knew they were rapidly nearing their destination. A happy smile brightened Jim's weathered features, as he finally continued.

"Well, the gal looks up at me with them big brown eyes. Nope, I'm wrong there. She give me another o' them penetratin' looks, like she's readin' my thoughts. Then she says to me, 'Jim, I hope I haven't misunderstood you.' 'Nope, you haven't,' says I, with a feelin' I shore never felt before. 'You know mighty well what I'm meanin',' I says.

"Then," he concluded, "we found a parson what was handy at tyin' a good tight knot. So you see, we didn't have much more'n time 'nough to notify *ourselves*, much. less our friends. Yep, that's the way it was. The ranch was sold, an' we found that little hideout." Jim was pointing to a rock house some distance from the road. It looked as though it might have grown from the side of the mountain.

"That's our nest," Jim said. "The end o' the windin' trail. An' we ain't aimin' to go no place now, 'cause we're as contented as a couple o' hummin'birds in a patch o' hollyhocks."